The Perspective

The Complex Morality of Defense and Firearms Ownership

Eric Greene

Table of Contents

Preface:

A Tale of Two Perspectives

On the evening of February 26, 2012, a seventeen-year-old named Trayvon Martin walked through a residential community in Sanford, Florida, returning from a convenience store with a bag of candy and a drink in hand. Before the night was over, he would be dead. The man who shot him, George Zimmerman, claimed he had acted in self-defense.

What followed was not merely a criminal investigation. It became one of the most emotionally charged public debates in modern American history. News outlets dissected every detail. Politicians weighed in. Protesters filled the streets. Millions of people formed conclusions, often long before the available facts could support them.

To some, Trayvon Martin was an innocent teenager whose life was unjustly taken. To others, George Zimmerman was a man who found himself in a violent confrontation and acted to preserve his own life.

To some, the case was primarily about race. To others, it was about the law of self-defense. To some, it exposed the dangers of armed citizens. To others, it reinforced the necessity of an individual's right to protect himself.

The same event. The same evidence. The same outcome.

Radically different conclusions. How is that possible? How can sincere, intelligent, well-intentioned people examine identical facts and arrive at entirely different understandings of what occurred?

That question—not the verdict, not the politics that grew up around it—is where this book actually begins.

Why This Book Had to Be Written

The purpose of *The Perspective* is not to relitigate the Zimmerman trial, nor to persuade the reader that one side of that controversy held a monopoly on truth. It is not an attempt to advance a political agenda in either direction. The case serves, instead, as a doorway into a far larger inquiry—one that extends well beyond a single neighborhood, a single confrontation, or a single verdict, into questions about human nature, morality, justice, and the responsibilities that accompany the power to protect life.

Modern conversations about firearms and self-defense are too often reduced to slogans, tribal affiliations, and emotional reflex. People are encouraged to choose sides rather than examine principles. Complex questions are compressed into simple categories, and nuance becomes the first casualty of certainty. Yet the underlying questions are anything but simple. What is the moral purpose of self-defense? When, if ever, is violence justified? Does the capacity to use force make a person dangerous, or does it make them capable of protecting the innocent? Is it more virtuous to be harmless, or to possess the capacity for force and exercise the restraint not to use it? What obligations accompany the right to bear arms? How should a society balance liberty with safety, justice with mercy, and the rights of the individual with the concerns of the community?

These questions have occupied philosophers, theologians, lawmakers, soldiers, and ordinary citizens for centuries. They are no less urgent now than they were thousands of years ago—and this book does not promise to resolve them. In many cases, no resolution exists that would survive serious scrutiny.

What it offers instead is a framework for thinking about them carefully—drawing on philosophy, theology, ethics, history, and law to explore what is actually at stake when a person is confronted with danger, responsibility, and the possibility of violence.

The goal is not to tell the reader what to conclude. It is to invite the reader to think more rigorously than the current public conversation typically allows.

In the pages that follow, you will encounter arguments you find persuasive and others you do not. That tension is intentional. Genuine growth rarely occurs when our existing beliefs are simply confirmed; it occurs when they are tested. The pursuit of moral clarity requires the humility to sit, however briefly, inside a perspective other than one's own.

Perhaps the most important lesson the Trayvon Martin case offers has little to do with its verdict and everything to do with what the public response revealed: that our understanding of events is shaped, often invisibly, by the assumptions, experiences, and values we bring to them before we ever encounter the facts. We do not simply observe reality. We interpret it. And those interpretations—formed long before any single case reaches the headlines—become the perspectives through which we define justice, assign responsibility, and decide who counts as victim, defender, aggressor, or hero.

Perspective is not a footnote to this discussion. It is the discussion. It determines how we judge the people involved in moments of violence, and it determines how each of us would act if we ever found ourselves standing where they stood.

At its core, this book asks one enduring question: *what moral obligations accompany the power to protect innocent life?* Everything that follows is an attempt to take that question as seriously as it deserves.

Whether you come to these pages as a firearm owner, a law enforcement officer, a member of the military, a student of philosophy, a person of faith, or simply a reader trying to think more clearly about a subject too often reduced to noise, my hope is that this book unsettles easy certainty on every side of the debate—including, where warranted, your own.

Because before we can understand justice, we must first understand responsibility. And before we can understand responsibility, we must first understand the perspective from which we are looking.

Every perspective begins with a question. This book is an attempt to ask it honestly.

Introduction:

Why Perspective Matters

Few subjects provoke more emotional certainty with less philosophical patience than the question of self-defense. Fewer still are discussed with such confidence by people who have never been forced to confront violence personally. Firearms ownership has become a kind of moral shorthand in modern culture—a signal, rather than a subject. To some, it communicates recklessness, aggression, and a certain political tribe. To others, responsibility, readiness, and a sober acknowledgment of the world's realities. What it rarely communicates, in the current climate, is what it actually is: a human response to vulnerability in a world that has never been as safe as it prefers to imagine.

This book exists because the conversation surrounding firearms has become intellectually shallow, morally inconsistent, and historically amnesiac. Arguments collapse into binaries—peace versus violence, compassion versus force, civilization versus arms—that are emotionally convenient and philosophically dishonest. They ignore thousands of years of moral reasoning, religious doctrine, and lived human experience that have treated self-defense not as an indulgence or a pathology but as a serious ethical responsibility governed by restraint, judgment, and conscience.

The question has never been whether violence should exist. It already does. The question—ancient, universal, and genuinely unavoidable—is whether a person may morally resist unjust aggression, and if so, by what means, under what conditions, and at what cost to the soul that chooses to act. Every civilization that has endured has answered that question. This book examines how they answered it, why those answers converge more than modern discourse admits, and what they demand of serious people today.

The Comfortable Contradiction

Modern discourse has developed a curious habit of treating firearms as a moral anomaly—an invention so uniquely corrupting that it somehow nullifies the ethical frameworks that predate it by millennia.

This reasoning collapses under minimal scrutiny. Tools change. Moral principles persist. A sword, a spear, and a firearm differ in efficiency and range, not in ethical category. What has always determined the morality of force is not the instrument, but the intent, the restraint, and the character of the person who wields it.

There is a deeper irony here, rarely acknowledged. Many who argue most forcefully against civilian firearms ownership do so while benefiting from layers of armed protection—police departments, military forces, private security, or the quiet deterrence created by others willing to stand between innocence and harm.

This outsourcing of moral burden produces a contradiction that deserves more honest examination than it typically receives. It is straightforward to condemn force in principle when one is effectively shielded from its absence in practice.

This book does not argue that firearms are inherently good. It argues something more difficult to dismiss: that the moral legitimacy of self-defense is embedded across religious, philosophical, and ethical traditions spanning continents and centuries; and that firearms, when oriented solely toward protection, are a modern expression of that enduring human principle.

When Ancient Traditions Speak With One Voice

One of the most instructive discoveries in cross-cultural moral study is how often traditions that disagree on nearly everything else arrive at similar conclusions on this. Judaism holds the preservation of life as a supreme obligation that can override almost every other consideration.

Christianity has wrestled for centuries with the tension between love, justice, and the legitimate use of force—and its mainstream traditions have not resolved that tension by declaring defense immoral. Islam permits force strictly to repel aggression while forbidding transgression in any form. Hinduism frames protection as a sacred duty when aligned with righteousness.

Buddhism, while placing non-harm at the center of ethical life, has long acknowledged the tragic necessity of defense in the protection of the innocent. Sikhism weaves spiritual discipline and the readiness to defend the oppressed into a single coherent identity.

These traditions do not agree on metaphysics, on salvation, or on much else. But on these points, their convergence is striking: life is sacred, injustice must be resisted, and restraint is the moral governor without which force becomes something else entirely.

That convergence is not a coincidence to be explained away. When diverse cultures, faiths, and philosophies—separated by geography, language, and centuries—arrive independently at similar moral conclusions, the burden of proof shifts.

The question is no longer whether self-defense belongs within the moral tradition of humanity. It clearly does. The question becomes how it must be practiced to remain worthy of that tradition.

The Equalizer and Its Demands

Firearms introduce no new moral category into human experience. What they alter is the balance of power—and that alteration is precisely where their moral significance lies. They allow the physically small to resist the strong, the elderly to resist the young, and the single to resist the many. This equalizing capacity is what unsettles critics most deeply, and it is also what has made firearms morally consequential in ways that blunt instruments rarely achieve.

But firearms also demand something that modern culture increasingly struggles to supply: genuine self-discipline. They expose the ego. They punish recklessness without warning.

They require emotional control, sustained training, and a sober, unromantic acceptance of consequence. Bearing arms is not empowering in the shallow way the word is usually meant. It is weighty. It asks something of the person who accepts it. Those unprepared to meet that moral gravity have no business accepting it—and the person who understands the burden most clearly is typically the least eager to deploy it.

The Argument This Book Makes

The thesis of this book is neither radical nor new. It is, in fact, ancient:

Across religious, philosophical, and ethical traditions, self-defense is recognized as morally legitimate when exercised with restraint and moral seriousness. Firearms ownership, when oriented exclusively toward protection rather than aggression, is a reasonable and defensible extension of humanity's enduring responsibility to preserve innocent life against unjust violence. This is not a claim of moral superiority over those who choose otherwise.

It is a claim of moral continuity—a recognition that the question being asked today is the same question every civilization before ours has been forced to answer. Firearms do not make a person righteous. Neither does refusing them confer virtue. What has always mattered—across traditions, across centuries, across every honest moral framework—is whether the individual bearing the capacity for force is also bearing the discipline, restraint, and conscience that alone can make that capacity something other than a danger.

This book does not begin with the question most people expect: *Do you support gun rights?* It begins with the question that actually matters—the one that predates every modern political argument by several thousand years:

What do we owe ourselves, and one another, when faced with unjust violence?

That question is where serious moral thinking begins. Everything else follows from this.

Perspective does not dissolve disagreement. But it does dissolve the kind of ignorance that masquerades as conviction. What follows is an exploration of conscience, tradition, and responsibility—one that treats firearms ownership not as a slogan to be defended or dismantled but as a genuine moral question that has been with us since the beginning, that will remain with us long after the current argument exhausts itself, and that deserves, at minimum, the dignity of serious thought.

The burden of that thought is real.

That is precisely why it cannot be avoided.

PART I

Framing the Moral Question

(Chapters 1-3)

The unexamined life is not worth living. — Socrates

Chapter 1:
Why Self-Defense Is a Universal Moral Question

Before there were governments, there were victims. Before there were courts, there was injustice. Before any civilization had codified a single law, human beings were already confronting the oldest moral emergency the species has ever faced: what to do when one person intends to destroy another who has done nothing to deserve it.

This is where the conversation about self-defense actually begins—not in a legislature, not in a constitutional convention, not in the aftermath of a modern tragedy, but in the deep, pre-political history of human vulnerability. The moral question of resistance did not arise because someone invented an efficient weapon.

It arose because human beings, from the earliest recoverable evidence of their existence, have been capable of deliberately harming one another—and because that capability immediately produced a problem that no amount of cultural sophistication has ever fully resolved.

Consider the most ordinary of moral scenarios: a mother alone with her children when someone forces entry into her home at night. She has no time to deliberate. No institution will arrive in time. The question she faces in that moment is not political, not ideological, not abstract. It is the oldest moral question the human species has ever produced—and the answer she must find is entirely her own. Self-defense, properly understood, is not an ideological position. It is an existential reality—one that morality becomes meaningful precisely by confronting.

The chapters of this book will examine how various religious, philosophical, and ethical traditions have grappled with that problem. But before those conversations can be had honestly, the foundational question must be addressed directly: why does self-defense persist as a moral question at all? The answer is that it persists because the conditions that produce it have never ceased to exist—and because the alternative to engaging with it seriously is not peace, but the quiet abdication of moral responsibility.

Violence as a Human Constant

The Evidence We Would Prefer to Forget

The archaeological record does not support a sentimental view of human prehistory. Long before the emergence of organized states, legal codes, or formal moral philosophy, human communities were engaging in lethal conflict at rates that would disturb any modern reader who encountered them honestly. Forensic analysis of prehistoric skeletal remains reveals patterns of trauma—cranial fractures, embedded projectile points, perimortem wounds—that speak not to isolated incidents but to recurring organized violence between groups (Walker, 2001). The ancient fortifications discovered at sites across Europe, the Near East, and Asia were not architectural flourishes. They were survival infrastructure, built by communities that understood, from direct and repeated experience, that the danger of violent incursion was real, persistent, and not amenable to wishful thinking (Arkush & Stanish, 2005).

The anthropologist Lawrence Keeley argued against what he called the "pacified past"—the comfortable modern assumption that violence is a corruption introduced by civilization rather than a problem civilization arose, in part, to manage (Keeley, 1996). His analysis produced a sobering conclusion: pre-state societies experienced rates of death from organized violence that, proportionally, exceeded those of the twentieth century, including its world wars. Civilization did not create the problem of violence. It inherited it, and then spent thousands of years developing moral, legal, and institutional structures in an attempt to contain it.

Those structures matter enormously. But they did not emerge from a vacuum of peaceable human nature suddenly disturbed by the invention of hierarchy and weapons. They emerged from the long, painful experience of communities that had learned—at considerable cost—what happens in the absence of organized moral and practical responses to aggression.

Why Violence Creates Moral Responsibility

The existence of violence in human experience is not, in itself, the moral problem. The moral problem emerges the moment a person of conscience asks, *what do I owe, to myself and to others, when I or they become the object of unjust aggression?*

This question is inescapable precisely because innocence is not a protection. The mother in that darkened hallway has done nothing to deserve her situation. Her children have done nothing. Their vulnerability is not a consequence of their choices—it is a consequence of someone else's. And yet the choices she makes in response to that vulnerability carry genuine moral weight.

Complete passivity in the face of violence directed at the innocent is not a morally neutral position. It is a decision, with consequences, for which the one who makes it bears some form of responsibility. The philosopher Jeff McMahan has argued that the moral asymmetry between aggressor and defender—between the person who initiates unjust violence and the person who resists it—is one of the most foundational distinctions in ethical theory (McMahan, 2009). To collapse that distinction in the name of a uniform rejection of force is not moral progress. It is moral evasion.

The relationship between vulnerability and responsibility runs deep in every serious ethical tradition. It is the recognition that we are not merely observers of injustice but potential agents within it—and that agency, once acknowledged, cannot be set aside without consequence.

The Illusion of Having Moved Beyond This

One of the more striking features of contemporary life in stable, prosperous societies is the ease with which large numbers of people can reach adulthood without ever having been seriously threatened with violence. This is, historically speaking, an unusual condition—one produced by layers of institutional infrastructure so reliable that they become effectively invisible to those they protect.

This psychological distance is understandable. It is also dangerous, in a specific and subtle way. People insulated from danger for long enough tend to mistake their insulation for a permanent feature of reality rather than a contingent achievement maintained by ongoing effort and, ultimately, by the credible capacity to respond to force with force when necessary.

As Michael Walzer observed, the peace enjoyed by civil societies is not self-sustaining—it rests upon structures of enforcement that are themselves expressions of organized, controlled force (Walzer, 1977). The police officer who never fires a weapon in thirty years of service is not evidence that force is unnecessary. Their presence is itself a form of deterrence—which is to say, a form of force held in reserve.

The ability to regard self-defense as a remote or distasteful topic is, therefore, a luxury purchased by the protective capacity of others. That luxury is not available to everyone. The single mother in a rural area, forty minutes from the nearest police station, navigating a genuine threat at two in the morning, does not have access to the comfortable abstraction that institutional safety makes possible for those who live within reach of it. For her, the moral problem addressed in this chapter has never been academic. Recognizing this does not require abandoning the aspiration toward peaceful civil order. It requires being honest about what that order actually rests upon.

Why Every Civilization Addressed Defense

The Question Was Never Whether Violence Existed

No serious ancient civilization operated under the illusion that violence could be wished away. The oldest legal codes in the historical record—Hammurabi's Code, the Laws of Ur-Nammu, the Twelve Tables of Rome—were not expressions of optimism about human nature (Roth, 1997). They were practical attempts to impose moral and legal structure upon a reality already understood to include conflict, aggression, predation, and the abuse of power. The existence of warrior classes in virtually every complex society is not evidence of cultural glorification of violence. It is evidence that communities understood the necessity of organized defensive capacity and developed moral frameworks to govern it.

Ancient fortifications tell the same story through a different medium. The walled cities of Mesopotamia, the hill forts of Iron Age Europe, and the defensive architecture of ancient China—these were expressions of the knowledge, acquired through experience, that communities without the capacity for defense did not endure (Trigger, 2003). Civilizations survived not by denying the reality of violence but by developing moral, legal, and practical structures capable of containing it.

The Architecture of Moral Restraint

What distinguishes the serious treatment of defensive force across cultures is not its celebration but its careful limitation. The concepts of proportionality, necessity, and restraint appear, in various formulations, across every major moral and legal tradition that has addressed the ethics of violence with any depth.

Roman law developed the principle of *vim vi repellere licet*—force may lawfully be repelled by force—but surrounded it immediately with qualifications: The response must be proportionate, immediate, and not motivated by vengeance (Watson, 1998). Medieval just war theory, developed most systematically by Thomas Aquinas, established criteria for legitimate force that remain recognizable in modern international law: just cause, right intention, proportionate means, and the principle that force must be a last resort rather than a first response (Aquinas, c. 1265–1274). These frameworks were not apologetics for violence. They were attempts to morally contain it—to draw the clearest possible line between force that serves justice and force that merely serves the interests, appetites, or grievances of the powerful.

The mother who defends her children does not act from appetite or grievance. She acts from the most morally coherent of motivations: the protection of innocent life that she is responsible for and that she loves. In the terms that Aquinas would have recognized immediately, her action—proportionate, necessary, directed at preservation rather than punishment—is precisely what the tradition of defensive ethics was designed to govern and affirm. The recurring appearance of these concepts across traditions separated by geography and centuries reflects the consistent moral intuition that while defensive force may sometimes be necessary, it is never simply permissible without condition.

The Universal Reach of the Problem

The religions and philosophies that will be examined in later chapters arrived at their positions on defensive force through very different theological and philosophical routes. But the fact that they all arrived at a position—that none of them simply ignored the question—is itself significant.

The Hebrew Bible's treatment of defensive killing distinguishes carefully between the innocent life lost in aggression and the life taken in genuine defense of the threatened (Telushkin, 1994). The Christian tradition's long engagement with just war theory reflects centuries of serious moral wrestling with the tension between the imperative of love and the reality of predatory evil (Augustine, c. 426 CE). Islamic jurisprudence developed sophisticated frameworks for distinguishing permitted defensive force from forbidden transgression, grounding the distinction in the Quranic principle that aggression must be resisted but not exceeded (Khadduri, 1955).

Hindu texts present the warrior's duty to protect the innocent as a sacred obligation—the abandonment of which is itself a moral failure (Doniger, 1991). Even Buddhist thought, with its profound commitment to non-harm, has produced serious ethical reflection on situations in which the protection of innocent life creates tragic moral necessity (Harvey, 2000).

The universality of this engagement does not prove that any single tradition's conclusions are correct. What it does prove is that the underlying problem is not culturally specific.

It is tied to the realities of human existence—to the fact that innocence is vulnerable, that predation is real, and that the question of moral response cannot be permanently deferred.

When Defensive Reality Is Ignored

The historical record is not kind to societies that convinced themselves the problem of violence had been transcended. The deliberate disarmament of populations by authoritarian regimes in the twentieth century did not produce safety—it produced dependency, and in the worst cases, facilitated atrocities that armed populations might have resisted more effectively (Rummel, 1994). The absence of defensive capacity does not eliminate violence. It redistributes the advantage it confers—invariably toward those willing to use force without moral restraint. Violence does not disappear when moral people refuse to engage with the ethics of resistance. It simply encounters less organized opposition.

Why Refusal to Discuss Defense Is a Modern Luxury

Distance as Distortion

The relative safety of modern liberal democracies has produced a cultural tendency to treat self-defense as a topic that decent people have moved beyond—a relic of less enlightened times, rendered unnecessary by the sophistication of institutional protection. This tendency conflates the experience of safety with the conditions that produce it and mistakes the absence of a visible threat for the absence of threat altogether. Geographic and institutional insulation from violence is real, and for those who live within it, it is genuinely valuable. But it is not uniformly distributed, and it is not permanent. The communities with the least access to reliable institutional protection have never had the luxury of treating defensive questions as abstract.

The single parent in an isolated location, the elderly person who cannot physically match the threat they face, the family in a neighborhood where response times exceed ten minutes—for these people, the moral problem addressed in this chapter has never been a matter of philosophical preference. It has been a matter of practical reality.

The Delegated Burden

Modern individuals in stable societies have largely delegated the responsibility of confronting violence to institutions—police, military, and security services—and this delegation is not inherently wrong. The difficulty arises when delegation becomes unconscious, and the awareness that someone, somewhere, is bearing the burden of confronting violence on everyone else's behalf fades from recognition entirely.

Institutions are composed of individual human beings who have chosen—in many cases at considerable personal risk—to place themselves between the public and the violence the public prefers not to think about. But those individuals cannot be everywhere.

The response time that separates a desperate phone call from actual assistance is a moral reality that comfortable abstract reasoning rarely acknowledges. The mother protecting her children does not have the luxury of waiting for theory to catch up with necessity. She has only the resources she has already accepted responsibility for carrying—and the courage to use them when nothing else remains.

Moral Seriousness Is Not Fascination With Force

Before this chapter concludes, one clarification is necessary. Engaging seriously with the ethics of self-defense is not the same as celebrating violence—and the distinction matters more than it might initially appear.

This book is not a militant text. It does not regard force as admirable, conflict as desirable, or the capacity for violence as a virtue in itself. What it regards as a virtue—and what the traditions examined in subsequent chapters consistently affirm—is the discipline, restraint, and moral seriousness with which the capacity for force is governed. The true moral danger is never force alone. It is force detached from accountability, proportionality, and the governing weight of conscience. A person who understands this distinction fully is far less likely to misuse capability than one who has never been asked to think about it at all.

Thoughts to Ponder: The Burden of Moral Agency

Self-defense persists as a moral question because the conditions that generate it—human vulnerability, the reality of predatory aggression, and the limits of institutional protection—have never ceased to exist.

Every civilization that examined these conditions seriously developed moral frameworks for addressing them, not because violence is desirable, but because the alternative—the surrender of the innocent to the unopposed aggressor—is morally untenable. The mother in the hallway is not a rhetorical device. She is the concrete, human face of a question that philosophy has addressed across millennia without fully resolving: what does a person of conscience owe to innocent life when institutions are absent and only their own capability and conscience remain? To reject, categorically and in advance, any moral legitimacy of defensive force is ultimately to answer that question with silence—and to leave the consequences of that silence with the people least able to absorb them.

This is not a celebration of force. It is a recognition that moral seriousness requires engaging with the world as it is, not only as we wish it to be. The burden of that engagement—its weight, its complexity, its resistance to easy resolution—is precisely what makes it a subject worthy of this book.

What the chapters that follow will not do is pretend the burden does not exist.

Chapter 2:

The False Binary—Peace or Violence

There is a habit of thought that dominates modern moral discourse on the subject of force, and it runs something like this: Violence is wrong, peace is right, and any person who takes seriously the possibility of defensive action has, in some meaningful sense, chosen the wrong side of that equation.

The appeal of this framing is obvious. It is clean, emotionally satisfying, and requires no difficult distinctions. It also happens to be philosophically incoherent.

The problem is not that the framing values peace—peace is worth valuing seriously. The problem is what the framing does to the category of force. By treating all uses of force as morally equivalent, it collapses a distinction that every serious ethical tradition in human history has regarded as foundational: the distinction between the person who initiates harm and the person who resists it. When that distinction disappears, moral reasoning does not become simpler. It becomes impossible.

Categories matter in ethics. A surgeon's blade and an assailant's knife are physically similar objects performing superficially similar acts, but no serious moral thinker would place them in the same category. What separates them is not the instrument but the intent, the context, the consequence, and the relationship between the person acting and the person affected.

The same principle applies to force. Force used to dominate is not the same moral act as force used to interrupt domination—and a framework that cannot acknowledge this difference is not a peaceful philosophy.

It is an incomplete one.

Why Peace and Violence Are Not Opposites in the Way Modern Culture Assumes

Peace Is Not the Absence of Force

Much of the confusion surrounding defensive force can be traced to a fundamental misunderstanding of what peace actually means—both historically and philosophically. The modern tendency is to define peace as the total absence of force, as though any use of coercive power, however bounded and however justified, represents a departure from the peaceful ideal. This definition is not only historically inaccurate. It is self-defeating.

The political philosopher Johan Galtung drew an important distinction between what he called "negative peace"—the mere absence of open conflict—and "positive peace," which involves the presence of justice, order, and functioning social institutions (Galtung, 1969). A community terrorized into silence is not at peace. A population so thoroughly dominated that resistance becomes unthinkable is not experiencing peace. It is experiencing the suppression that precedes a different kind of violence.

Historically, stable peace has never been understood as the elimination of all force from social life. It has been understood as the ordering of force—its subjection to law, accountability, and moral constraint. Courts issue judgments. Police enforce them. None of this is violence in the morally significant sense. All of it involves force. The difference is not the presence or absence of coercive power—it is what that power serves and how it is constrained.

A peaceful society, properly understood, is not one in which force has been abolished. It is one in which unjust force is restrained—and in which those capable of restraining it are willing to do so.

Violence Is Defined by Purpose, Not Mere Action

If peace is not the absence of all force, then violence cannot be defined simply as the presence of it. A definition of violence that encompasses every use of physical force places the aggressor and the defender in the same moral category—and that placement systematically advantages the person willing to initiate harm and disadvantages the person attempting to stop it.

The moral character of a physical act cannot be determined by the act alone. Intention matters. Initiation matters. Proportionality matters. The relationship between the parties, the circumstances that produced the confrontation, and the consequences that flow from action and inaction all enter into any honest moral assessment (Walzer, 1977). A strike delivered in rage at an innocent person and a strike delivered to stop an assault already in progress are not the same act, wearing different justifications. They are different acts, separated by the entire moral distance between predation and protection.

This is the consistent position of virtually every serious moral tradition in recorded history. The Roman legal concept of *vim vi repellere licet*—force may lawfully be used to repel force—was not a license for aggression masquerading as defense. It was a precise moral and legal distinction, carefully bounded by conditions of proportionality and necessity (Watson, 1998).

The tradition of just war theory developed the same insight at greater length across centuries of philosophical and theological reflection.

What unites these traditions is the shared recognition that the moral character of force is determined not by its physical nature but by its purpose, its constraints, and its relationship to the injustice it either perpetrates or resists.

Why Defensive Force Occupies a Separate Moral Category

Defense is, by definition, reactive. It does not create the moral crisis it responds to. It does not initiate the harm it seeks to interrupt. Its purpose is not conquest or domination—it is the preservation of what the aggressor is attempting to destroy.

Michael Walzer articulated this with characteristic precision: the aggressor, by initiating unjust violence, forfeits the moral protections that ordinarily govern how others may treat them (Walzer, 1977). The defender, by contrast, has done nothing to generate their situation. Their use of force, constrained by necessity and proportionality, is not a departure from the moral order. It is an attempt to restore it. Defense exists because peace is fragile—because it can be violated—and the willingness to acknowledge that fragility is not a concession to militarism. It is a condition of moral honesty.

The Moral Failure of Flattening Aggressor and Defender Into the Same Category

Why Moral Context Is Not Optional

Human moral systems have always evaluated actions contextually. This is not a weakness of ethical reasoning—it is one of its most important strengths.

The capacity to distinguish between a doctor who causes pain in the course of healing and a torturer who causes pain for its own sake is not sophistry. It is the recognition that human actions acquire their moral meaning from the full constellation of circumstances in which they occur.

Aristotle argued that virtue is not a fixed behavior but a disposition exercised well, and that exercising it well requires the judgment to assess particular situations accurately (Aristotle, trans. 2009). Abstract rules, applied without contextual judgment, produce moral outcomes often worse than the harm they were designed to prevent. The command "never use force" sounds simple and principled. Applied to a situation in which force is the only available means of preventing a greater harm—a parent watching a child be attacked, a bystander witnessing an assault—it produces not virtue but complicity: the complicity of the person who preferred moral tidiness to moral responsibility.

The Difference Between Initiating Harm and Interrupting Harm

The moral difference between aggression and defense is not merely a matter of sequence, though sequence carries ethical weight. It is a difference in the fundamental orientation of the act toward the other person involved. Aggression treats the victim as an object—something to be dominated or destroyed for the aggressor's purposes. Defense treats the aggressor's victim as a subject—a person whose life and safety possess value worth protecting, even at cost to the defender.

The aggressor bears full responsibility for creating the circumstances that make defensive force necessary. They have introduced the moral emergency. The defender, responding with proportionate and necessary force, has not chosen to be in a moral crisis.

They have been placed in this moral crisis by another person's decision. A moral framework that acknowledges this distribution of responsibility can adequately protect the innocent; therefore, the burden of initiation belongs to the one who initiated it (McMahan, 2009).

Why Moral Flattening Benefits Aggressors

The practical consequences of collapsing the moral distinction between aggressor and defender are not evenly distributed. When a society is unable to distinguish between initiating harm and resisting it, two things happen simultaneously: The aggressor loses moral accountability, and the defender loses moral legitimacy. The aggressor benefits from this arrangement. The defender does not.

History provides illustrations that are difficult to dismiss. Authoritarian regimes disarmed populations and denied them the moral and practical capacity for resistance, so these populations did not experience the equality of the unarmed. They experienced the radical vulnerability of those who could be harmed without consequence (Rummel, 1994). Criminal behavior at every scale depends upon an asymmetry of willingness—the willingness of the predator to use force against a target unable or morally prohibited from responding in kind. A society that cannot distinguish between the predator and the person resisting predation lacks moral clarity. It has achieved a form of moral confusion that reliably advantages the former.

The Ethical Cost of Absolute Pacifist Framing

This is not an argument against pacifism as a personal moral commitment. There are serious, thoughtful people who have adopted absolute non-violence as a way of life and accepted its costs with genuine integrity.

What does not deserve the same respect is the application of pacifist moral logic to situations affecting others, particularly vulnerable others who have not chosen and cannot escape the circumstances in which they find themselves.

The parent who refuses to use any force to prevent a child from being harmed is not making a morally serious decision. They are making a morally comfortable one—one that preserves their own sense of principled innocence at the cost of the child's safety. Moral seriousness, as Bernard Williams observed, sometimes requires making choices that are genuinely tragic—choices between imperfect options in which every available path carries some moral cost (Williams, 1981). The refusal to choose, or the choice of inaction dressed as principle, does not escape the tragedy. It simply relocates its costs onto those least able to bear them.

Defense as the Moral Interruption of Injustice

Injustice Is Active, Not Passive

Injustice, once initiated, does not pause out of courtesy while its targets deliberate. Harm advances unless interrupted. Predatory behavior, at every scale from the interpersonal to the geopolitical, expands when it encounters no resistance and contracts when it does. Any moral framework that fails to account for this pattern is building on demonstrably false premises.

Defense is the establishment of a moral boundary that aggression seeks to erase. The aggressor's act is an implicit claim: that the victim's well-being, safety, and life are available for the aggressor's purposes. The defender's response is the refusal of that claim—the assertion, enacted rather than merely stated, that the victim's life possesses a value the aggressor is not permitted to override. Understood in these terms, defensive force is not the abandonment of moral order. It is one of the ways moral order defends itself against those who would destroy it.

Why Defense Is Fundamentally About Limitation

The moral legitimacy of defensive force does not arise from its effectiveness alone. It arises from its character—and that character is defined, above all, by limitation. This is why the just war tradition insisted so carefully on the conditions under which force could be legitimately used—not to make defense more difficult, but to ensure that the force deployed in defense of justice did not itself become a new form of injustice (Aquinas, c. 1265–1274).

Proportionality demands that the response not exceed what is necessary to stop the harm. Necessity demands that less harmful alternatives be exhausted or unavailable before force is employed. Last resort insists that force is not a first option but a reluctant one, chosen when other means have failed. These constraints are not bureaucratic obstacles. They are the moral structure that distinguishes defense from retaliation, protection from punishment, and the interruption of harm from its continuation by other means.

The Tragic Nature of Defensive Force

Any honest treatment of defensive force must acknowledge what serious moral traditions have consistently recognized: that the legitimate use of force, even in genuine defense of innocent life, is not a triumph.

It is a tragedy—morally, psychologically, and humanly costly in ways that do not dissolve simply because the cause was just. The person who has used force to protect a loved one does not, if they are morally serious, experience the aftermath as uncomplicated. The psychological literature on post-traumatic responses among those who have employed defensive force reflects this moral weight with consistent clarity (Grossman, 1995). The weight is not evidence that the action was wrong. It is evidence that the person who took it understood what it cost—and that understanding is itself a mark of moral seriousness rather than its absence.

Why Refusing to Interrupt Injustice Is Not Morally Neutral

Inaction is not moral neutrality. When injustice is in motion and a person with the capacity to interrupt it chooses not to, that choice has consequences—consequences that fall upon the victim rather than upon the person who declined to act. As the ethicist Jonathan Glover observed, the history of atrocity is not only a history of people who did terrible things—it is substantially a history of people who stood by while terrible things were done, and who found ways to regard their passivity as something other than what it was (Glover, 1999). Neutrality in the presence of aggression does not distribute its moral costs equally. It distributes them toward the victim.

Thoughts to Ponder: Peace Requires Boundaries

The argument this chapter has developed is not a celebration of force. It is a defense of moral clarity—the clarity without which force cannot be evaluated, justified, condemned, or constrained. Peace and violence are not simple opposites. Defensive force differs morally from aggression in ways that matter profoundly for how societies protect the innocent while preserving their own ethical integrity.

A society unwilling to interrupt injustice does not transcend violence. It merely surrenders the initiative to those willing to use force without restraint, without conscience, and without the moral limitations that defensive ethics have always demanded. That surrender is not peace. It is the precondition for a different kind of harm—one made possible by the absence of any serious willingness to resist it.

If defensive force can be morally legitimate—if the distinction between aggression and defense is as foundational as the traditions examined here suggest—then the question that follows is immediate: where exactly does morality reside in this picture? Is it in the tool? In the law? Or in something that precedes both—in the character, conscience, and formation of the person who must ultimately decide?

Chapter 3:

Tools, Intent, and Moral Agency

There is a recurring temptation in moral discourse to locate responsibility in the wrong place—to fix blame upon an object, a system, or an abstraction rather than upon the human being whose choices actually determined the outcome. This temptation is understandable. Objects cannot argue back. They sit in courtrooms as silent evidence, in newspaper photographs as stark symbols, and in political debates as convenient focal points for anxieties that are, at their root, anxieties about human nature. Blaming the tool is, in a very real psychological sense, easier than confronting the person who wielded it.

But moral reasoning built on convenience rather than accuracy does not produce clarity. It produces confusion—and in this particular domain, that confusion has consequences. When a society assigns moral agency to objects rather than to persons, it lets the guilty escape the full weight of their responsibility while burdening the innocent with the implied guilt of mere possession.

It redirects ethical energy away from the questions that actually matter—questions about character, formation, restraint, and the conditions under which human beings make destructive choices—toward questions that cannot bear the full moral weight being placed upon them.

Tools have no will. A firearm lying on a table is neither dangerous nor safe, neither moral nor immoral. It is inert—a physical object whose ethical significance is entirely dependent upon the human being who picks it up, the intention that person brings to the act, and the judgment they exercise in every moment that follows.

Morality cannot reside in steel and polymer. It can only reside in persons.

Tools Have Never Possessed Morality

The Difference Between Instrument and Intention

The philosophical distinction between a tool and the intention behind its use is among the oldest and most persistent recognitions in the history of moral thought. Aristotle, developing his account of human action and responsibility in the *Nicomachean Ethics*, understood that the moral evaluation of any act requires identifying the agent—the deliberating, choosing, intending person—whose decision set events in motion (Aristotle, trans. 2009).

Without a moral agent, there is no moral act. There is only the operation of physical causation, which belongs to science rather than ethics.

A tool extends the reach of human will. It amplifies consequences and alters the practical relationship between intention and outcome. But it cannot generate moral purpose independently. The firearm discharges because a human finger applies pressure to a trigger in pursuit of a human aim. The moral character of the act—its justness or injustness, its necessity or recklessness—traces entirely to the human being at its origin.

The capacity for restraint—for the decision not to act, or not yet, or not with the degree of force initially contemplated—belongs entirely to the agent. The tool cannot second-guess, hesitate, or stand down.

Only the person holding it can do those things, which means that the moral weight of every outcome belongs, fundamentally and inescapably, to the person who chose.

Why Human Societies Historically Understood This Clearly

Ancient and medieval societies were, in many respects, clearer on this point than modern culture tends to be. The codes of conduct that governed warriors across cultures—from the Homeric tradition of honorable combat to the chivalric codes of medieval Europe, from the Bushido tradition of feudal Japan to the warrior ethics embedded in Hindu texts—were not primarily concerned with the weapons themselves (Friday, 1997). They were concerned with the character of the person bearing them.

Warrior codes regulated behavior rather than armament because the people who developed them understood where the actual moral danger resided. The sword of an honorable man and the sword of a treacherous one were physically identical objects. What distinguished their use was the moral formation—or its absence—in the hands that held them.

Hunting traditions across cultures developed elaborate protocols governing how animals could be taken—not because the bow or the spear was inherently problematic, but because the act of taking life was understood to be morally significant and therefore subject to moral governance (Ortega y Gasset, 1972).

The consistent pattern across these traditions is the direction of moral attention: toward the person, not the implement. Misuse of a weapon reflected a failure of character rather than a corruption inherent in the tool itself.

Why Technological Advancement Intensified Moral Confusion

If earlier societies were relatively clear on this point, why has modern culture become so confused? Part of the answer lies in the nature of technological advancement itself.

As tools become more efficient—as the scale of potential harm increases and the physical demands required to inflict damage decrease—the psychological discomfort surrounding those tools increases proportionally.

This discomfort is not irrational. More efficient tools do produce more severe consequences when misused, and the awareness of that severity naturally colors moral perception.

But there is a crucial difference between acknowledging that powerful tools demand greater moral seriousness and concluding that the tools themselves are the source of the moral problem.

The historian Barbara Tuchman observed this pattern repeatedly in her examination of how societies respond to technological change—displacing anxieties about human behavior onto the instruments through which that behavior is expressed (Tuchman, 1984). Efficiency changes consequences.

It does not change the ethical structure. The moral questions that governed the use of a spear—is this force defensive? Is it necessary? Is it proportionate?—are precisely the moral questions that govern the use of a firearm.

Technology has altered the scale and speed at which these questions must be answered. It has not altered the questions themselves.

Firearms Exist Within a Historical Continuum of Defensive Tools

Every Era Developed Tools for Protection

The history of human material culture is, among other things, a continuous record of the development of protective technology. From the earliest worked flints serving as both hunting implements and defensive weapons through the progression of spears, shields, swords, bows, and armor, human communities in every recoverable era have invested significant resources in developing more effective means of protecting themselves from violence (Keeley, 1996).

This investment was not the expression of a uniquely violent impulse. It was the practical response of communities that understood, from experience, that the desire to live in safety must be backed by the capacity to resist those who would violate it.

The moral reasoning accompanying this development was embedded in the cultures that produced it. Societies developed rules governing when defensive tools could be used, against whom, under what circumstances, and with what limitations.

The existence of those rules is evidence not of indifference to the moral significance of violence but of sustained engagement with it. Firearms belong to this continuum. They did not introduce violence or its associated moral problems into human experience. They introduced a new level of efficiency into an old equation whose fundamental moral structure had been debated and refined across centuries before the first firearm was ever discharged.

Historical Moral Anxiety About New Weapons Is Not New

One of the more instructive patterns in the history of weaponry is the remarkable consistency with which each new development in military technology provoked moral anxiety. The longbow was condemned by some medieval commentators as unchivalric, undermining the moral order of honorable combat (Prestwich, 1996). The crossbow was explicitly condemned by the Second Lateran Council in 1139 on the grounds that it was too lethal and too easily operated (Contamine, 1984). The introduction of firearms in the fifteenth and sixteenth centuries produced similar objections—that they democratized killing in ways that violated established moral hierarchies and placed destructive capacity in the hands of people insufficiently formed to bear it responsibly.

Each generation, encountering a new level of destructive efficiency, has been tempted to locate the moral problem in the technology rather than in the human condition that was present before the technology existed and remains present after it. This pattern does not prove that concerns about any specific technology are always misplaced. It does suggest that the reflex to blame the instrument is consistent enough across history to warrant skepticism—and that the more useful question is never simply what the tool can do, but what the person holding it has been formed to do with it.

Why Firearms Differ in Capability, Not Moral Category

The practical differences between firearms and earlier defensive tools are real and should not be minimized. Firearms operate at greater distances, require less physical strength, and produce consequences that are more immediately severe and less reversible than those of earlier weapons. These differences matter for questions of policy, training, and legal governance. They do not alter the fundamental moral structure within which all uses of defensive force must be evaluated.

Jeff McMahan, in his careful analysis of the ethics of killing in defense, identifies the morally relevant questions as ones of necessity, proportionality, and the moral relationship between the parties involved—questions applying with equal force regardless of the specific instrument through which defensive action is taken (McMahan, 2009). Is the threat genuine? Is the defensive response necessary? Is the force proportionate? Is the person using force the defender rather than the initiator of the moral crisis? These questions governed the ethics of armed defense when the relevant instrument was a spear. Technological changes do not alter the moral principles by which actions are evaluated.

Why Firearms Intensify Modern Psychological Discomfort

The irreversibility of a firearm's discharge—the compressed interval between decision and lethal consequence—forces a confrontation with moral responsibility that slower, more physically demanding instruments allowed people to evade or experience more gradually. This confrontation is, in a philosophical sense, clarifying rather than distorting. Firearms insist upon the concreteness of moral choice and the permanence of its consequences.

The psychologist David Grossman, in his extensive research on the psychological dimensions of killing, observed that the moral and psychological burden associated with taking human life reflects the depth of the human aversion to harming others—an aversion that, far from being eliminated by the availability of efficient weapons, is actually intensified by the knowledge of their power (Grossman, 1995). The discomfort many people feel in the presence of firearms is not evidence of the weapons' inherent corruption. It may, paradoxically, be evidence of precisely the moral seriousness that their responsible possession demands.

Moral Legitimacy Depends Upon Governance, Not Objects

Why Defensive Tools Require Moral Formation

The greater the capability a tool confers, the greater the moral burden placed upon the person who holds it. This principle is embedded in virtually every tradition that has reflected seriously on the relationship between power and responsibility. The Roman concept of *gravitas*, the Stoic emphasis on self-mastery, the warrior codes of feudal Japan, the chivalric traditions of medieval Europe—all reflect the consistent recognition that powerful tools require formed persons to govern them (Nitobe, 1900). Capability in the absence of moral formation is not neutral. It is dangerous in direct proportion to the efficiency of the instrument it accompanies.

This is why serious traditions of firearms ownership have always emphasized training, discipline, and the cultivation of judgment alongside technical proficiency. The technical capacity to operate a firearm accurately is necessary but far from sufficient as a moral preparation for bearing one. What is additionally required is the formation of inner governance—the restraint, the contextual judgment, and the emotional control—that determines whether technical capacity is deployed wisely, reluctantly, and proportionately; or recklessly, eagerly, and without adequate regard for consequence.

Internal and External Governance

The governance of powerful tools operates at two levels, both necessary and incapable of substituting for the other. External governance—laws, regulations, training requirements, and accountability structures—provides the social framework within which individuals exercise their choices. It establishes boundaries and creates consequences for their violation. This external governance is legitimate and important.

But external governance, however well designed, cannot reach into the moment of decision. It cannot be present in the critical seconds during which a person holding a firearm must determine whether the circumstances justify its use, whether the threat is genuine, and whether alternatives have been genuinely exhausted. Those determinations are made by the internal governance of conscience, restraint, and formed moral judgment—capacities that law can encourage but cannot create (Aristotle, trans. 2009). As John Locke observed, the ultimate foundation of civil order is not the law itself but the moral character of the persons who compose the civil community—without which law becomes an external shell surrounding a void (Locke, 1689).

Moral societies require both dimensions operating together. The danger arises from their separation—from external rules being present while internal character is absent, or from confident moral character operating without accountability structures to correct its errors.

Why Focusing Solely on Tools Distracts From Character

The cultural habit of centering debates about violence on instruments rather than on persons is not merely a philosophical error.

It is a practical one with measurable consequences. When moral and political energy focuses primarily on the tool, the deeper questions—about the formation of character, the cultivation of judgment, the development of emotional regulation, and the social conditions under which people acquire the moral resources necessary for responsible behavior—receive less sustained attention than they deserve.

These deeper questions are harder. They resist the simplicity of legislative solutions. They implicate institutions—families, schools, communities, religious traditions—whose influence over individual moral formation is real but diffuse and long-term.

As Aristotle recognized, virtue is not instilled by instruction alone—it is formed through practice, through the habitual exercise of judgment under conditions that gradually develop the moral reflexes upon which good behavior under pressure depends (Aristotle, trans. 2009). Recklessness with a firearm is not produced by the firearm. It is produced by the absence of the patience, humility, and self-awareness that responsible use demands—and that absence is a character failure, not a design flaw.

Firearms as Revealing Rather Than Corrupting

Firearms do not create the moral qualities of the people who bear them—they reveal those qualities with unusual clarity and speed. The reckless person who handles a firearm recklessly is not made reckless by the weapon. The careful, disciplined person who handles it with the gravity it demands is not made careful by it. The firearm accelerates the expression of already-present moral qualities because its consequences are immediate, severe, and largely irreversible—leaving little room for the casual thoughtlessness that other domains of life sometimes absorb without catastrophic results.

The moral danger lies not in capability itself, but in capability detached from the restraint and conscience that alone can govern it responsibly. Where that restraint is present, a firearm is a morally serious tool in the hands of a morally serious person. Where it is absent, the problem is not the tool. The problem is the person—and the conditions, both personal and social, that failed to form them adequately for the responsibility they accepted.

Thoughts to Ponder: The Moral Center of Self-Defense

Morality cannot reside in objects. It can only reside in persons—in the intentions they bring to their actions, the judgment they exercise in their choices, the restraint they maintain under pressure, and the conscience that governs them when no external authority is present to enforce compliance.

Firearms belong within the long continuum of defensive instruments that human beings have developed across their history. Their greater efficiency places greater moral demands upon those who bear them—demands for training, discipline, emotional control, and the sober acceptance of consequence that serious capability requires. But the moral framework within which those demands make sense is not new. It is the same framework that governed the sword, the spear, and every other instrument through which human beings have sought to protect themselves from unjust violence.

If responsibility belongs to the individual moral agent—as this chapter has argued it does—then a foundational question immediately presents itself. Where does that agent's right to act in self-preservation actually originate? Is it granted by the state? Does it derive from social convention? Or does it arise from something deeper—something that precedes law, precedes government, and precedes the particular historical moment in which any given person finds themselves confronting the question?

That is the question Chapter 4 will address.

PART II

Philosophy & Ethics of Force

(Chapters 4-7)

The supreme art of war is to subdue the enemy without fighting.
— Sun Tzu

Chapter 4:

Natural Law and the Right to Preserve Life

A person standing in the path of violence does not pause to consult a legal code before deciding whether their life is worth protecting. They do not wait for institutional permission to experience the recognition that what is happening to them is wrong, that the harm approaching them is unjust, and that their survival possesses a value that the aggressor has no legitimate claim to destroy.

This recognition—immediate, pre-reflective, and universal—is not a product of any particular legal system or political tradition. It is something older, deeper, and more fundamental than any document a government has ever produced.

This is the starting point of natural law thinking, and it is a starting point with significant implications for the ethics of self-defense. If the right to preserve life were merely a privilege granted by political authority, it would follow that political authority could revoke it—that governments could, with sufficient democratic consensus or sufficient power, render the innocent obligated to submit to their own destruction.

Most serious moral traditions have found this conclusion unacceptable, not because it is politically inconvenient but because it is philosophically incoherent. A right that exists only by permission is not a right.

It is a temporary accommodation, revocable at will, whose moral status is entirely dependent upon the goodwill of whoever holds power at any given moment.

Natural Law and the Moral Reality of Self-Preservation

What Natural Law Attempts to Explain

Natural law is not a single unified theory but a broad family of moral and philosophical frameworks united by a common premise: that some moral truths exist independently of human legislation and can be discovered through reason, reflection upon human nature, and careful attention to the conditions of human flourishing.

The tradition reaches from ancient Stoic philosophy through the medieval synthesis of Thomas Aquinas, into the Enlightenment political philosophy of John Locke, and continues to inform contemporary legal and moral debate in ways that often go unacknowledged (Finnis, 1980).

The natural law tradition does not claim to invent morality. It claims to recognize moral realities that are already embedded in the structure of human existence—realities that any sufficiently careful and honest observer can, in principle, discover.

The convergence of independent moral traditions on similar conclusions—the consistent recognition, across cultures and centuries, of the value of human life, the legitimacy of its defense, and the necessity of restraint in the exercise of force—is taken as evidence that these conclusions reflect something real about the human condition rather than merely the preferences of particular societies at particular moments (George, 1992).

This matters for the ethics of self-defense in a specific and important way. If the legitimacy of defending human life is a natural moral reality rather than a social construction, then its authority does not depend upon the political context in which any given person finds themselves.

It cannot be legislated out of existence without simultaneously legislating away the moral foundations upon which all other rights depend.

Why Self-Preservation Is a Pre-Political Reality

The impulse toward self-preservation is among the most universal features of human experience across every culture and historical period for which records exist. This universality is not, by itself, a moral argument—many impulses are universal without being morally significant.

What elevates self-preservation from a mere biological drive to a moral claim is the recognition that it is inseparable from the possession of a life that possesses intrinsic value.

John Locke, whose political philosophy exercised enormous influence on the development of modern democratic institutions, grounded the right of self-preservation in the prior fact of human beings possessing lives that belong, in a morally significant sense, to themselves (Locke, 1689).

This is not merely the assertion that people want to survive—it is the claim that human life carries a moral weight that cannot be overridden without justification, and that the unjust taking of that life represents a violation of something real and significant, not merely the frustration of a preference.

Aquinas, approaching the same question from a theological rather than a political direction, argued that the inclination to preserve one's own life reflects a participation in the rational order of creation—that self-preservation, properly ordered and morally governed, is not merely permissible but is expressive of the right relationship between a person and the life they have been given (Aquinas, c. 1265–1274). The specific theological framework differs from Locke's secular one, but the underlying moral conclusion is strikingly similar: the right to preserve life is not a grant from any human authority.

It is a recognition of a moral reality that human authorities did not create and cannot legitimately destroy.

Why Rights Must Precede Governments

The logic of natural law has direct implications for the relationship between individuals and the political institutions that govern them. If rights—including the right to self-preservation—exist only because governments choose to recognize them, then they are not rights at all. They are permissions. And permissions, unlike rights, can be withdrawn.

The history of the twentieth century offers sufficiently grim illustrations of what follows when political authority is understood to be the source of human rights rather than their guardian.

Governments that claimed the authority to define who possessed the right to life and who did not were not operating outside any theoretical framework—they were operating within a framework that denied the pre-political moral status of the individual and treated human worth as a political determination (Rummel, 1994).

The natural law tradition's insistence that governments arise to secure preexisting rights rather than to manufacture human dignity is not a philosophical abstraction. It is a conclusion drawn from the most serious moral reflection on what happens when that insistence is abandoned.

The Right to Preserve Life Does Not Mean Unlimited Force

Why Natural Law Rejects Both Passivity and Excess

The natural law tradition's affirmation of the right to self-preservation is not an endorsement of unlimited force. This point deserves emphasis, because the most common misreadings of natural law arguments in the context of self-defense tend to push in one of two directions—either toward the conclusion that natural law justifies any degree of violence undertaken in the name of survival, or toward the conclusion that a consistent pacifism is the only morally coherent position available. Natural law, properly understood, rejects both.

Aquinas was explicit on this point. In his treatment of self-defense in the *Summa Theologica*, he argued that defensive force is morally legitimate but subject to the condition of proportionality—that the force employed must not exceed what is necessary to accomplish the defensive purpose (Aquinas, c. 1265–1274).

This is not a bureaucratic qualification attached reluctantly to an otherwise unlimited right. It is an expression of the underlying moral logic: the right to self-preservation is grounded in the value of human life—including, crucially, the life of the aggressor, who retains their human nature even while forfeiting certain protections through their own unjust conduct.

The moral framework that justifies defense also imposes limits upon it, and those limits are not separable from the justification without destroying the moral coherence of the entire position.

The Difference Between Preservation and Revenge

Among the most important distinctions that natural law thinking draws in the domain of defensive force is the distinction between self-preservation and revenge.

They may, in specific circumstances, involve similar outward actions. They differ entirely in their moral orientation—and that difference is, within the natural law framework, morally decisive.

Self-preservation is future-directed. It aims at stopping an unjust harm that is currently in motion or immediately imminent. Its purpose is the continuation of innocent life, not the punishment of the aggressor, the satisfaction of wounded pride, or the restoration of a sense of power or control that violence has temporarily disrupted. Revenge, by contrast, is past-directed.

It responds not to a present threat but to a prior injury, seeking satisfaction rather than safety. The Stoic philosophers, whose influence on the development of natural law thinking was substantial, were particularly clear on the danger of allowing anger to govern the use of force—not because anger is always irrational, but because anger oriented toward the past cannot reliably produce the disciplined, proportionate, future-directed response that genuine defense requires (Seneca, trans. 2004).

The same moral framework that permits defensive force explicitly forbids its use as an instrument of emotional satisfaction or punitive retaliation.

This is not a minor qualification. It is the distinction between a moral agent exercising a legitimate right under genuine necessity and a person using the vocabulary of defense to justify what is, in moral substance, something else entirely.

Why Moral Equality Matters

One of the most significant features of the natural law framework for thinking about self-defense is its insistence on the equal moral worth of all human beings. The right to self-preservation is not reserved for the physically strong, the socially powerful, or the institutionally protected. It belongs, equally and without qualification, to every person whose life possesses intrinsic value—which, within the natural law framework, means every person without exception.

This has practical implications that are not always acknowledged in debates about defensive capacity. A moral right that cannot be exercised is, in practice, no right at all. The elderly person threatened by a physically stronger aggressor, the individual confronted by multiple attackers, the person in a remote location where institutional assistance cannot arrive in time—these are not marginal cases that natural law thinking can afford to ignore. They are precisely the cases in which the gap between a formally recognized right and a practically exercisable one becomes most visible and most morally significant (Lott, 2000).

The natural law tradition grounds the right to self-defense in moral equality—in the equal worth of every human life—rather than in physical capability or social status. This grounding has implications for the question of effective defensive means that the tradition cannot consistently avoid. A moral framework that affirms the equal right to preservation while remaining indifferent to whether that right can be practically exercised by the vulnerable has not fully followed its own logic.

Why Effective Means of Defense Matter Morally

The point that follows from the preceding argument is neither aggressive nor politically pointed. It is simply the observation that rights require practical content to be more than formal declarations. The natural law tradition has consistently recognized that moral obligations and moral rights have real-world dimensions—that affirming a person's right to preserve their life while systematically denying them access to effective means of doing so creates a tension within the moral framework that cannot be resolved by simply insisting upon the formal recognition of the right.

This does not constitute an argument for the unlimited distribution of any particular tool. It is an argument for taking the relationship between moral rights and their practical conditions of exercise seriously—for acknowledging that the defense of the physically vulnerable against the physically powerful is a genuine moral concern that the ethics of self-defense cannot responsibly set aside (Kleck, 1997).

Governments Recognize the Right to Preserve Life; They Do Not Create It

Why Governments Exist, and What They Cannot Replace

Political authority, within the natural law tradition, is not self-justifying. Governments exist because the moral problems they address—the coordination of social life, the adjudication of disputes, the protection of individuals from the predatory behavior of others—preceded them. They are responses to moral realities that were already present in human experience before any government was formed to manage them. This means that their authority is instrumental rather than absolute—they exist to serve the conditions of human flourishing, and their legitimacy depends upon how faithfully they do so (Locke, 1689). This has a specific implication for the question of self-defense: institutional protection, however valuable and however robust, is not a substitute for the underlying right to preserve life. It is one means—a socially organized and generally superior means—by which that right is given practical expression. When institutional means are available and effective, their use is generally preferable. But the availability of institutional protection does not extinguish the underlying right, and the unavailability of that protection does not suspend it.

Why Institutional Protection Has Limits

Law enforcement agencies operate under constraints of geography, resources, and response time that no amount of institutional competence or political will can entirely eliminate. Studies of emergency response patterns consistently confirm what anyone with practical experience of emergency situations already understands: in the critical moments when violence is occurring, institutional assistance is frequently unavailable (Kleck, 1997). This is not a criticism of law enforcement—it is an acknowledgment of the structural reality within which all institutional protection operates.

When systems fail—when institutions are overwhelmed, when geography places people beyond the reach of timely response, when social order collapses under conditions of disaster or civil unrest—the underlying moral right to preserve life does not fail with them. It persists because it was never dependent upon institutional functioning in the first place. Natural law thinking maintains that the individual, in the absence of available institutional protection, retains the full moral right to defend their life with whatever means are available and proportionate to the threat they face. The state's failure to protect does not transform the person being attacked into someone obligated to accept that attack without resistance.

Why Dependency Alone Cannot Sustain Moral Agency

The natural law tradition's account of political authority does not treat individuals as passive recipients of institutional protection whose moral agency is fully discharged once they have complied with applicable laws and regulations. It treats them as moral agents who retain personal responsibility for their choices and their consequences, even within the context of organized social life. This retention of moral agency is not incidental—it is one of the features of the natural law framework that most clearly distinguishes it from approaches that locate all moral responsibility in collective institutions.

The complete outsourcing of defensive responsibility to institutions is, within this framework, not a morally neutral position. It involves the tacit abdication of a form of personal responsibility that the natural law tradition regards as inalienable—the responsibility of a moral agent for their own preservation and, in appropriate circumstances, for the preservation of those entrusted to their care. This abdication may be comfortable. It is not, on serious examination, coherent.

Firearms Within the Natural Law Framework

Firearms, within the natural law framework, occupy a straightforward moral position: they are instruments that may be employed in the service of an already-existing moral right. They do not create that right. They do not alter its fundamental moral structure. They do not change the conditions—necessity, proportionality, defensive intent, restraint—under which force is morally legitimate. What they potentially do is make the practical exercise of the right to self-preservation more accessible to people who would otherwise be at a severe disadvantage in confrontations with more physically powerful aggressors. The moral evaluation of any specific use of a firearm in a defensive context must, within the natural law framework, be conducted in terms of those same foundational conditions. Was the threat genuine? Was defensive force necessary? Was the response proportionate? Was the intent preservative rather than punitive?

These are not questions that the technology answers. They are questions that the moral agent must answer—and the quality of those answers depends not upon the instrument but upon the character, judgment, and restraint of the person who bears it.

Thoughts to Ponder: Rights Rooted in Reality

The right to preserve life is foundational because life itself is foundational. It does not depend upon the political arrangements of any particular era for its validity, because its roots run deeper than political arrangements—into the pre-political moral reality of human beings who possess lives of intrinsic worth and who face the enduring possibility of those lives being unjustly threatened.

Governments that function well acknowledge this right and work to create conditions in which its exercise is rarely necessary. Governments that function poorly remind us, through the vulnerability they expose, that the right existed before they did and persists when they fail. The natural law tradition's insistence upon the pre-political character of self-preservation is not an argument against political authority. It is an argument for political authority properly ordered—authority that understands itself as the guardian of rights it did not create and cannot legitimately destroy.

A society that denies the moral legitimacy of preserving innocent life does not achieve a higher form of civilization. It removes the moral foundation upon which all other rights depend and leaves the vulnerable with no recourse but to hope that the powerful choose, on any given day, to exercise their power with restraint. That hope is not a moral framework. It is an abdication of one.

Chapter 5:
Stoicism, Duty, and Controlled Force

Most philosophies offer some version of comfort. They promise meaning, or transcendence, or the assurance that the universe is, at some level, arranged in humanity's favor. Stoicism offers none of these things. It begins, instead, with a proposition that is bracing precisely because it refuses the consolations that other systems extend:

The world is indifferent to human preference, unpredictable in its demands, and entirely capable of placing a person in circumstances for which no amount of wishful thinking provides adequate preparation.

This is not pessimism. It is the foundational act of philosophical honesty from which everything else in the Stoic tradition follows.

What Stoicism offers in place of comfort is something more durable and, ultimately, more useful: a method. Not a method for controlling external events—the Stoics were explicit that such control is not within human power—but a method for governing oneself within those events with clarity, discipline, and integrity. The Stoic philosopher does not ask how the world might be arranged to produce less suffering. He asks how a person of reason and virtue should conduct himself when suffering arrives regardless.

This distinction between what can be controlled and what cannot is not a minor philosophical preference. It is the structural foundation of an entire moral psychology—one with direct and serious implications for the ethics of force, defense, and the character required to bear both responsibly.

Stoicism and the Discipline of Internal Governance

The Stoic Distinction Between Control and Circumstance

The foundational distinction in Stoic philosophy—the axis around which the entire tradition rotates—is the division between what lies within our control and what does not. Epictetus, the former slave whose *Discourses* remain among the most searching documents in the history of moral philosophy, articulated this division with characteristic directness: some things are up to us, and some things are not (Epictetus, trans. 2008).

What is up to us—our judgments, our intentions, our responses, and our conduct—constitutes the entire domain of moral life. What is not up to us—the behavior of others, the contingencies of circumstance, the arrival of danger or injustice—is beyond the reach of virtue to prevent, though never beyond the reach of virtue to address.

This distinction has a consequence that is easily misread. It does not mean that external events are morally irrelevant or that the Stoic simply accepts whatever happens without response.

It means that the response—its character, its discipline, its proportionality, its governance by reason rather than by impulse—is where moral life actually resides. Marcus Aurelius, whose *Meditations* record a sustained private effort to apply Stoic principles under conditions of extraordinary pressure and responsibility, returned repeatedly to the recognition that the quality of a life is measured not by what it encounters but by what it brings to those encounters (Aurelius, trans. 2006). The emperor who governed an empire while confronting military threats, political betrayal, personal grief, and the daily temptations of absolute power understood, with unusual clarity, that the governing of oneself was the more demanding and more important task.

Acceptance, within the Stoic framework, is not resignation. It is the refusal of illusion—the unwillingness to waste moral energy on demanding that the world be other than it is, directed instead toward the question of what reason and virtue require within the world as it actually presents itself.

Why Stoicism Rejects Emotional Extremes

The Stoic treatment of emotion is among the most frequently misunderstood aspects of the tradition, partly because of the word "stoic" in its popular usage, which has come to suggest emotional suppression or cold indifference. The Stoics did not advocate the elimination of feeling. They advocated the governance of feeling—the refusal to allow emotional states, however understandable, to make decisions that reason should be making instead (Graver, 2007).

This distinction matters enormously in the context of force and defense. Anger, fear, and the desire for revenge are not simply irrational—they can be responses to genuine injustice, legitimate threats, and real violations of what matters.

The Stoic does not deny this. What the Stoic insists upon is that these emotional responses, however legitimate in origin, are unreliable guides to action precisely when the stakes are highest. Anger compresses judgment. Fear distorts assessment. The desire for revenge reorients the purpose of force away from the protection of the innocent and toward the satisfaction of ego—and that reorientation, as the tradition consistently emphasized, is among the most reliable paths to moral failure even when the cause was initially just. Seneca, whose essays on anger represent some of the most psychologically acute writing the ancient world produced, argued that rage is not merely an unpleasant emotion but a cognitively corrupting one—that it systematically produces inaccurate assessments of situations, inflated estimates of threat, and an appetite for responses that exceed what genuine necessity could ever justify (Seneca, trans. 2010).

The person who acts from anger rather than from reasoned judgment is not exercising force. They are being exercised by it.

Virtue as Operational Discipline

The four cardinal virtues of the Stoic tradition—wisdom, courage, justice, and temperance—are not ornamental moral qualities to be admired from a distance. They are operational capacities, developed through sustained practice, that determine the quality of a person's conduct under conditions of genuine pressure. The tradition was explicit that these virtues are interdependent: the absence of any one of them corrupts the exercise of the others in ways that produce moral failure rather than moral achievement.

Courage without wisdom becomes recklessness—the willingness to act decisively in situations that actually demand patience, negotiation, or restraint. Justice without courage becomes passivity—the clear perception of what is right, paralyzed by the unwillingness to accept the personal cost of acting upon that perception. Temperance without resolve becomes avoidance—the preference for emotional equilibrium over the difficult demands of genuine duty. Wisdom without the courage to act upon it remains merely theoretical, a moral understanding that makes no difference to the world it accurately describes (Hadot, 1998).

What emerges from this interdependence is a picture of virtue not as a set of abstract commitments but as a form of disciplined readiness—the capacity to perceive accurately, respond proportionately, act when action is genuinely required, and restrain when restraint is what justice demands. This is, among other things, precisely the character that the responsible exercise of defensive force requires.

Duty, Responsibility, and the Moral Failure of Passivity

Why Stoicism Does Not Equate Virtue With Harmlessness

One of the most important correctives that Stoic ethics offers to certain strands of contemporary moral thinking is its refusal to identify goodness with incapacity. The Stoic tradition does not regard a person's inability to exercise force as morally equivalent to the disciplined choice not to exercise it. These are entirely different conditions, and confusing them produces a moral category error with practical consequences.

A person who is incapable of violence is not demonstrating restraint. They are simply operating at the limits of their physical or practical capability. Restraint—moral restraint, the kind that carries genuine ethical weight—requires the actual capacity to act differently, and the disciplined choice not to.

The value is in the governance of power, not in the absence of it. As Pierre Hadot observed in his study of Marcus Aurelius's philosophical practice, the Stoic ideal is not the person who lacks the capacity for harm but the person who possesses it and has brought it under the governance of reason and duty

(Hadot, 1998). Harmlessness achieved through weakness is not virtue. It is merely a different kind of vulnerability.

Why Inaction Can Become Moral Failure

The Stoic framework recognizes, with unusual clarity, that inaction carries moral weight just as action does. The refusal to act is itself a choice—one with consequences that fall upon other people, often people who are vulnerable precisely because those with the capacity to help them have declined to exercise it. Epictetus was direct about the moral significance of this: the Stoic is not free to claim virtue while permitting preventable injustice to proceed on the grounds that intervention would be personally costly or emotionally uncomfortable (Epictetus, trans. 2008).

This is the Stoic response to what contemporary philosophy sometimes calls the bystander problem—the moral situation of a person who possesses the capacity to prevent harm but chooses, for reasons of comfort, convenience, or ideological purity, not to act. The Stoic analysis is unsparing: the question to be asked is not what keeps the person emotionally comfortable, but what reasoned duty requires, given their actual circumstances and actual capabilities. Comfort is not a moral criterion. The tradition that produced Marcus Aurelius—a man who spent significant portions of his reign on military campaigns he did not want, because duty required it—had no patience for moral positions whose primary virtue was their immunity to personal inconvenience.

Duty Flows From Role and Capacity

Stoic ethics recognizes that moral responsibility is not uniformly distributed. It varies with role, with relationship, and with capability—and this variation is not an inconsistency but a feature of a moral framework sophisticated enough to reflect the actual structure of human life. A parent bears specific responsibilities toward a child that strangers do not. A person with the capacity to interrupt harm bears a different set of obligations than a person without it. A leader bears responsibilities toward those in their charge that private individuals do not share in the same degree (Long, 2002).

This differentiation of responsibility has a specific implication for the ethics of defense and preparedness. The person who has developed the capability to respond effectively to violence—through training, through discipline, through the cultivation of the self-command that effective response requires—has not merely acquired a tool. They have acquired a form of responsibility. The capability is inseparable from the obligation to exercise it wisely, to deploy it only when genuine necessity requires, to restrain it when circumstances do not warrant its use, and to bear the full moral weight of every decision made in its name.

Preparedness, within this framework, is not aggression held in reserve. It is a responsibility taken seriously—the recognition that the possibility of danger is real, that the capacity to respond to it effectively is a form of moral seriousness, and that developing that capacity without simultaneously developing the character to govern it would be something considerably more dangerous than ignorance.

Why Stoicism Rejects Dependency Disguised as Moral Idealism

Among the less comfortable observations that Stoic ethics makes about contemporary moral life is its implicit challenge to positions that present dependency upon institutional protection as a form of principled commitment to non-violence. The Stoic analysis recognizes that many modern moral claims about the illegitimacy of defensive force depend, at their foundation, upon the continuous availability of institutional alternatives—police, security systems, and the reliable presence of organized protective capacity. Remove that availability, and the moral position that seemed principled becomes something closer to a luxury assumption.

This is not an argument against institutional protection. It is an argument for honesty about the conditions under which certain moral positions are sustainable. Stoicism prepares individuals for the possibility that responsibility may arrive personally, suddenly, and in circumstances for which no institutional response is available. The tradition regarded this preparation not as paranoia but as the appropriate response of a rational person to an honest assessment of what the world is actually capable of producing.

Controlled Force and the Ethics of Self-Command

Why Stoicism Evaluates Force Rather Than Condemning It Absolutely

The Stoic tradition does not treat force as inherently virtuous or inherently corrupt. It treats force as a morally serious capacity whose ethical character is entirely determined by the discipline, intention, and governance brought to its exercise. This position is neither a license for aggression nor a prohibition on defense. It is a framework for moral evaluation—one that asks, in every particular case, whether the force being contemplated meets the standards of necessity, proportionality, and rational governance that legitimate defensive action requires (Sellars, 2006).

Necessity demands that the force be genuinely required—that less harmful alternatives have been exhausted or are genuinely unavailable. Proportionality demands that the response bear a reasonable relationship to the threat, not exceeding what the actual situation warrants. Rational governance demands that the decision be made by reason rather than by the emotional state of the moment—by the calm, clear assessment of what the situation actually requires rather than by what anger, fear, or wounded pride is currently demanding.

Controlled force, meeting these conditions, may be morally justified within the Stoic framework. Force that fails them—however emotionally compelling the circumstances that produced it—cannot claim the moral legitimacy that genuine defense possesses.

The Difference Between Preparedness and Aggression

The Stoic conception of defensive preparedness is not the anticipatory aggression that critics of armed readiness sometimes imagine it to be. It is closer to what athletes and emergency professionals understand as trained calm—the development of practiced competence and emotional regulation specifically so that pressure and danger do not produce the panic, the tunnel vision, and the loss of judgment that untrained responses to crisis typically exhibit.

Marcus Aurelius, writing to himself in the *Meditations*, reflected on the importance of preparation not as the accumulation of strategic advantage but as the cultivation of the internal resources necessary for rational conduct under conditions that would, without preparation, overwhelm reason entirely (Aurelius, trans. 2006). The Stoic prepares precisely so that the moment of crisis does not become the moment of moral failure—so that the decision made under pressure reflects the values cultivated in quieter moments rather than the unexamined impulses of a mind that has been overtaken by its own fear or rage.

Firearms Through a Stoic Lens

The Stoic framework applied to firearms produces a perspective that is neither celebratory nor dismissive. Firearms are not symbols of power, identity, or political belonging—the Stoic tradition has limited patience for the attachment of moral significance to external objects of any kind. They are serious instruments with serious consequences, and their possession demands the serious character that serious consequences require.

What the Stoic framework insists upon, above all else, is the subordination of the instrument to the discipline of the person who bears it. The danger in any powerful tool is never primarily the tool itself—it is the absence of the self-command, the restraint, and the formed moral judgment that responsible use requires.

Bravado is a form of emotional excess, and the Stoic tradition treats emotional excess as a moral failing regardless of the direction it takes. The person who carries a firearm as an expression of toughness, dominance, or ideological identity has already failed the most basic test that Stoic ethics applies: the test of whether the instrument serves reason and duty or whether it serves the ego instead (Robertson, 2019).

The Emotional Aftermath of Defensive Force

The Stoic tradition's insistence on emotional governance does not produce indifference to the consequences of force—and this point deserves particular emphasis, because the Stoic ideal is sometimes mistaken for a kind of moral coldness that the tradition itself would have rejected. Stoicism acknowledges that even justified force—force that was genuinely necessary, properly proportionate, and rationally governed—may leave behind emotional and moral residue that the person who exercised it is responsible for confronting honestly.

Sorrow at having been placed in a situation where defense was necessary is not weakness. Reflection upon the cost of what occurred, even when what occurred was morally justified, is not irrationality. What Stoicism forbids is the emotional excess in either direction—neither the pride that regards the exercise of lethal force as an achievement to be celebrated, nor the irrational guilt that treats the legitimate defense of innocent life as though it were equivalent to aggression (Graver, 2007). The appropriate response is something more measured: the acknowledgment of tragedy without chaos, the acceptance of moral weight without self-destruction, and the continued commitment to the discipline and restraint that prevented a difficult situation from becoming something worse.

Thoughts to Ponder: Strength Governed by Reason

The Stoic does not seek conflict. He prepares for the possibility that conflict may seek him, and he prepares not by cultivating aggression but by cultivating self-command, clarity of judgment, and moral formation that would prevent a moment of genuine crisis from becoming a moment of moral failure. The strength the tradition commends is not the strength that seeks occasions to demonstrate itself. It is the strength that holds itself in reserve, governed by reason and duty, until reason and duty together determine that restraint is no longer morally possible.

Strength becomes morally dangerous only when it is detached from reason, from discipline, and from the accountability that the Stoic tradition regards as inseparable from genuine virtue. Attached to those things—formed by them, governed by them, expressed through them—it is not something to be feared. It is something that the protection of innocent life, in a world that has never guaranteed anyone's safety, sometimes requires.

This raises the question that the following chapter must address directly.

Chapter 6: Pacifism and the Burden of Moral Responsibility

Pacifism deserves to be taken seriously. This is not a concession made reluctantly before an argument designed to dismantle it—it is a starting point that honest engagement requires.

The pacifist tradition, in its most serious forms, is not motivated by naivety.

It is motivated by a genuine and morally weighty recognition: that violence is costly, that its costs are frequently underestimated by those not bearing them, and that the glorification of force has produced some of the worst chapters in human history.

These concerns are not only understandable but also valid. They are correct. Any serious treatment of defensive ethics that does not acknowledge them has not engaged fully with the problem it claims to address.

The disagreement between pacifism and the traditions examined in preceding chapters is not about whether violence is serious.

It is about whether seriousness alone is a sufficient moral response to injustice already in motion—and whether a commitment to personal non-resistance, however admirable in origin, can sustain its moral character when innocent people are in immediate danger.

The Moral Tension Within Absolute Pacifism

Why Pacifism Appeals Morally

The moral appeal of pacifism is genuine, and understanding it clearly is a prerequisite for engaging with its limitations honestly. At its most serious, pacifism represents a sustained recognition that human beings are capable of convincing themselves that almost any violence is justified—that the history of force is substantially a history of rationalizations, in which necessity and defense have been stretched to cover acts driven by pride, revenge, or the appetite for domination.

The philosopher Jenny Teichman observed that one of pacifism's most important moral functions is its insistence that the burden of proof lies with those who would employ force—that violence is not a morally neutral option but a morally serious act requiring compelling justification (Teichman, 1986).

This insistence is right. The traditions of just war theory and natural law thinking would agree with it. The problem arises not with the demand for justification but with what pacifism does when justification genuinely exists—when necessity, proportionality, and defensive intent are present, and the threat to innocent life is real and immediate.

The Difference Between Moral Intention and Moral Outcome

Good intentions and positive outcomes are not the same thing. The moral quality of an act cannot be determined solely by the internal state of the person performing it, without reference to its consequences for those affected. Even traditions primarily focused on duty and character have consistently recognized that moral responsibility extends beyond the management of one's own conscience to include the effects of one's choices on others (Mill, 1863).

This has a direct implication for absolute pacifism. A person who refuses force under any circumstances can achieve a form of personal moral purity—they can honestly claim never to have contributed to violence. But if that refusal permits preventable harm to fall upon innocent people depending upon them for protection, the purity they have preserved is purchased at someone else's expense.

The question ethics must ask is whether that transaction—personal innocence maintained at the cost of preventable suffering transferred to others—represents genuine moral achievement or a sophisticated form of moral self-interest.

The Problem of Absolute Non-Resistance

Absolute pacifism faces its most serious challenge not in philosophical abstraction but in concrete cases where its application produces the starkest moral results. The parent who watches a child being harmed and refuses intervention on principled grounds has not demonstrated moral purity.

They have demonstrated that commitment to a principle carries greater weight, in their moral calculus, than the immediate welfare of the person they were responsible for protecting.

The philosopher Jeff McMahan argues that absolute non-resistance fails not because it values peace incorrectly, but because it applies that value without adequate attention to the moral claims of those whose lives are immediately at stake (McMahan, 2002).

A moral framework that produces, as its practical consequence, the protection of the aggressor's unimpeded access to innocent victims has not achieved ethical refinement. It has inverted the moral priorities that the protection of human dignity was supposed to express.

Why Injustice Does Not Depend Upon Moral Approval

The most persistent structural weakness of absolute pacifism is its implicit assumption that principled non-resistance will somehow be recognized or reciprocated by those whose conduct it refuses to resist. Predatory behavior does not require moral justification to proceed. It requires opportunity. As Michael Walzer observed, the restraint of the peaceful does not produce restraint in those with no interest in peace—it produces the asymmetry of capability that aggressive actors exploit with historically consistent regularity (Walzer, 1977).

A moral philosophy designed for a world where aggressors respond to non-resistance with restraint may be adequate for that world. It is not adequate for the one that actually exists.

Moral Responsibility and the Duty to Protect

Why Moral Responsibility Extends Beyond the Self

Ethics is not primarily the management of personal innocence. It is the negotiation of responsibility within webs of relationship—toward family, community, and the vulnerable whose welfare may depend upon the choices of people with the capacity to affect their situation. Aristotle's account of virtue understood human beings as inherently social and moral life as inherently relational—the virtuous person engages with difficult situations through wisdom, courage, and restraint, accepting the burden of moral complexity rather than purchasing comfort through avoidance (Aristotle, trans. 2009).

The most morally serious cases for defensive force are rarely about personal survival alone. They are about the protection of those who cannot protect themselves, and a moral framework that has no adequate response to their situation has not fully discharged its ethical obligations.

Why Capability Creates Obligation

Virtually every serious moral tradition has recognized that moral obligations are shaped, at least in part, by what a person is capable of doing—that the one who possesses the means to prevent harm and the one who does not, are not in identical moral positions (Singer, 1972). The person who has cultivated the capability to respond effectively to genuine threat has entered into a different moral relationship with situations where that capability becomes relevant. Capability does not inherently corrupt. It intensifies the responsibility to exercise wisely what one has developed.

The Difference Between Harmlessness and Virtue

Among the more consequential confusions in contemporary moral culture is the persistent equation of harmlessness with goodness—the implicit assumption that the absence of the capacity for force is itself a moral achievement. Genuine virtue is not demonstrated by the inability to act otherwise.

It is demonstrated by the disciplined choice to act well among the full range of options available. As Pierre Hadot observed in his study of Stoic practice, the moral ideal is not the person who lacks the capacity for harm but the person who possesses it and has brought it under the governance of reason and duty (Hadot, 1998).

Restraint—moral restraint of the kind that carries genuine ethical weight—requires the actual capacity to act differently, and the disciplined choice not to. The development of defensive capability, undertaken with moral seriousness and governed by appropriate restraint, is not a departure from virtue. It is, in the appropriate circumstances, one of its expressions.

Why Outsourced Responsibility Creates Ethical Contradictions

There is a tension embedded in many pacifist positions that deserves more honest examination than it typically receives. Most people who adopt non-resistance as a personal moral commitment do not actually live in a world without defensive force—they live in a world where defensive force is exercised on their behalf by police, military personnel, and others who have accepted the responsibility that others have declined.

The philosopher Cheyney Ryan raised this point in his examination of pacifist ethics: that a moral position sustained by others' willingness to confront violence cannot claim the universal moral authority to which absolute pacifism aspires (Ryan, 1983).

The burden of confronting violence is not eliminated by refusing to share it. It is transferred silently, without acknowledgment, to those willing to bear it.

Defense as Compassion Under Pressure

Why Defense Emerges From Moral Concern for Others

The framing that presents defensive force as the opposite of compassion misunderstands both. Compassion is not the commitment to personal non-involvement in suffering—it is the genuine concern for the welfare of others that motivates action on their behalf, including action that involves moral burden and the exercise of force.

The parent who places themselves between a child and harm is not departing from love. They are expressing it in the form the circumstances demand.

Nel Noddings, in her development of care ethics, argued that genuine care for others is not expressed through withdrawal from situations requiring difficult engagement but through responsive action oriented toward the actual needs of those being cared for (Noddings, 1984).

Abstract commitment to nonviolence, maintained at the cost of specific vulnerable people suffering preventable harm, is not the expression of care. It is the substitution of an ideological commitment for the relational responsibility that care actually requires.

Defense of the innocent—constrained by necessity, proportionality, and the intention to preserve rather than to dominate—is not a departure from compassion.

It is one of the forms compassion takes when circumstances make its more comfortable expressions inadequate.

Firearms and the Burden of Explicit Capability

Firearms are morally distinctive not primarily in their capacity for harm but in the explicitness with which they confront their possessor with the reality of defensive capability.

A firearm is a continuous, concrete reminder that its bearer has accepted a particular form of moral responsibility—one with immediate, irreversible consequences if exercised and potentially significant consequences for others if not exercised when genuine necessity required it.

This explicitness is uncomfortable, and the discomfort is not unreasonable. But the discomfort of acknowledged responsibility is not an argument against responsibility—it is one of the conditions under which serious moral formation occurs. The moral burden lies not in the capability itself but in whether that capability is governed by conscience, restrained by proportionality, and directed by genuine concern for the welfare of others.

Why Moral Seriousness Requires Difficult Choices

The most mature moral traditions have consistently recognized that ethical life does not present itself primarily as a series of clear choices between good and evil. It presents itself, far more often, as a series of genuine dilemmas in which every available course of action carries moral cost. Bernard Williams captured this precisely: the person who insists on finding a morally unambiguous position in every situation has not achieved greater ethical refinement—they have achieved a less honest relationship with the complexity that actual circumstances produce (Williams, 1981). The situation in which defensive force is genuinely necessary rarely offers the option of clean hands.

It offers the option of bearing the moral weight of difficult action or of transferring the consequences of inaction onto those least able to bear them. Mature ethics accepts this tension rather than dissolving it through the expedient of a principle that places personal purity above the welfare of vulnerable others.

Peace as Something That Must Sometimes Be Defended

Peace is not a state that sustains itself through the mere desire for it. It is a condition that requires, among other things, the practical capacity to resist those who would violate it—and the moral willingness to exercise that capacity when the violation is real, immediate, and not amenable to less costly responses. This is not the endorsement of a militarized society or the casual normalization of defensive violence. It is the recognition that aspiration and capability are not substitutes for each other.

The historical record, examined honestly, suggests that moral order endures not merely because people aspire to it but because some are willing, when necessary, to protect it—to stand in the space between the innocent and those who would harm them, bearing the burden that such standing requires. This willingness is not the abandonment of the commitment to peace. It is one of the conditions under which peace remains more than a fragile hope.

Thoughts to Ponder: Responsibility Without Brutality

Pacifism asks a question that every serious moral tradition must be willing to answer honestly: what is the cost of force, and who bears it? It is right to insist that this cost is real, that it is frequently underestimated, and that the history of justified violence contains enough unjustified violence to warrant permanent moral suspicion of the rationalizations through which force presents itself as necessary.

But the question that pacifism must in turn answer is this: what is the cost of non-resistance, and who bears that cost? If the answer is that the cost falls primarily upon the innocent who cannot protect themselves, then a moral framework that refuses to confront this outcome in the name of principled purity has not resolved the ethical problem. It has displaced the ethical problem silently, and it has done so at the expense of those least able to absorb its consequences.

Compassion and defensive responsibility are not opposites. They are moral tensions that a complete ethical framework must hold in productive balance—refusing the brutality that force without restraint produces while refusing equally the comfortable fiction that non-resistance maintained at others' expense constitutes an adequate response to injustice already in motion. Peace endures not through wishful thinking alone. It endures when compassion is paired with responsibility, when restraint governs capability, and when the willingness to protect innocent life is regarded not as a departure from moral seriousness but as one of its most demanding expressions.

If defensive force may sometimes be morally necessary, the question that immediately follows is consequential: How can it remain morally limited? What are the boundaries separating legitimate defense from excess, necessary force from retaliation, and protection of the innocent from the satisfaction of the ego that protection too easily becomes? That is the question the next chapter will address.

Chapter 7:
Proportionality and Moral Restraint

The moment a defensive force loses its boundaries, it loses its moral character. What separates legitimate defense from mere violence is not the presence of provocation—provocation can be invented or exaggerated—but the discipline with which force is governed once it begins. Without that discipline, defense collapses into vengeance, and the person who began as a victim becomes, by degrees, something the moral framework of defense can no longer coherently protect.

Proportionality and restraint are not qualifications attached reluctantly to the right of self-defense. They are the conditions without which that right ceases to be a right and becomes an excuse.

Understanding Proportionality Beyond Simplistic Symmetry

Why Proportionality Is Often Misunderstood

Few concepts in the ethics of defensive force are more consistently misapplied than proportionality. In popular moral discourse, the term tends to be understood as aesthetic symmetry—the intuition that the response to violence should mirror the violence that provoked it, that equal force represents moral balance, and that any response exceeding the apparent scale of the threat has overstepped its justification. This understanding is not merely imprecise.

It is actively misleading, and its application to real defensive situations produces moral judgments bearing little relationship to the ethical questions actually at stake.

The just war tradition, which developed the most sustained philosophical treatment of proportionality in the Western moral canon, understood the concept in fundamentally different terms. Proportionality concerns the relationship between force employed and harm it is directed at preventing, not the visual or emotional symmetry between attack and response (Walzer, 1977). The defender's obligation is to use the force genuinely necessary to stop the unjust harm being perpetrated. That obligation does not include accepting disadvantage to satisfy an observer's retrospective sense of fair play.

The problem of retrospective moral judgment is particularly acute in defensive situations. Those who assess defensive force after the fact possess information unavailable to the defender at the moment of decision—they know how the situation resolved, what the aggressor's actual capabilities were, and whether the threat was as serious as the defender perceived. The defender possessed none of this. They possessed only a rapid, imperfect, stress-compromised assessment of an immediate threat—and the moral evaluation of their response must account for the conditions under which that assessment was made, rather than substituting the calm retrospective judgment that the moment itself did not allow (McMahan, 2009).

Why Defenders Are Not Morally Required to Accept Disadvantage

Proportionality is also sometimes misread as requiring the defender to place themselves at a deliberate disadvantage—to use less effective means, to hesitate when hesitation increases risk, or to calibrate their response to the aggressor's apparent capability rather than the genuine requirements of stopping the harm. This position sounds principled. Examined carefully, it is not.

The innocent person being attacked has done nothing to generate their situation. The moral burden belongs entirely to the aggressor who initiated it. To require the defender to weaken their response in the name of fairness toward that aggressor—a person who has forfeited significant moral protections through their own unjust conduct—is to redistribute moral consideration in precisely the wrong direction.

As McMahan argues, the moral asymmetry between unjust aggressor and innocent defender is one of the most foundational distinctions in ethical theory, and collapsing it in the name of symmetry produces conclusions no coherent moral framework can sustain (McMahan, 2009).

Proportionality does not require equal force. It requires justified force—genuinely directed at stopping the threat, constrained by the actual requirements of that purpose, and not extended beyond what those requirements demand.

The Relationship Between Necessity and Moral Legitimacy

Necessity operates as the primary moral boundary on defensive force. Force is morally legitimate when genuinely required to stop unjust harm—and only then.

This condition is not satisfied by the mere existence of threat. It is satisfied when the specific force employed is the minimum reasonably required to address the threat under actual circumstances present.

Necessity imposes a direction on defensive force that distinguishes it fundamentally from retaliation.

Retaliation is oriented toward the past—toward harm already occurred and the emotional need to answer it. Necessity is oriented toward the present—toward harm currently in motion that must be stopped. Force extending beyond what necessity requires, from stopping a threat to punishing an aggressor, has exceeded the moral boundary that necessity defines (Finnis, 1980).

The moral question necessity poses is not "how much force was used?" but "was the force necessary to stop the threat?" These are different questions with different moral implications, and substituting the first for the second is among the most common sources of confused ethical judgment in discussions of defensive force.

Why Context Matters Morally

Ethical judgment that ignores context is not rigorous—it is abstraction pretending to be rigor. Fear affects perception. Stress compresses time and narrows attention.

The rapid assessment that defensive situations demand does not occur under laboratory conditions—it occurs in the presence of genuine danger, genuine uncertainty, and genuine consequences for error in either direction.

The defender who misjudges the severity of a threat under these conditions is not in the same moral position as a person making the same misjudgment in comfort and safety.

Acknowledging this does not eliminate accountability. It defines what realistic moral accountability for decisions made under genuine pressure actually looks like (Grossman, 1995).

Restraint as Strength Rather Than Weakness

Why Restraint Requires Strength

The persistent association of restraint with weakness represents one of the more damaging misunderstandings in popular thinking about force.

Unrestrained reaction requires nothing—it is the path of least psychological resistance, the surrender to whatever emotional state the moment has produced.

Measured, disciplined response under conditions of genuine threat and emotional pressure is among the most demanding things a human being can be asked to do.

It requires the simultaneous management of fear, rapid assessment of complex circumstances, suppression of retaliatory impulses, and the disciplined application of force calibrated to genuine necessity rather than emotional intensity.

Marcus Aurelius, whose *Meditations* record a sustained private effort to apply Stoic principles under conditions of extraordinary pressure, consistently returned to the recognition that self-command—the governance of one's own responses under conditions inviting excess—is not the absence of strength but its highest expression (Aurelius, trans. 2006).

Restraint, properly understood, is not what prevents a person from acting effectively. It is what ensures that when they act, their action serves the purpose that moral legitimacy requires.

The Difference Between Controlled Force and Emotional Force

Defensive force loses its moral character—gradually, and then decisively—when its governance passes from reason to emotion. Anger, fear, and wounded pride are not experiences that announce themselves as corrupting influences. They present as urgency, as righteous indignation, and as the reasonable demand that injustice receive an adequate answer. Their effect on moral judgment is nevertheless consistent: they inflate the perceived severity of threat, compress assessment of alternatives, and generate appetite for responses exceeding what genuine necessity could ever justify (Seneca, trans. 2010).

The defender who acts from discipline asks, in every moment that force continues, is this still necessary? Is this still proportionate? Is this still directed at stopping harm rather than satisfying the emotional residue of having been threatened? These are not questions that anger asks. They require the emotional governance that the Stoic tradition called self-command and that just war theory embedded in the concept of right intention—the requirement that force serve the moral purpose justifying it, rather than the emotional purposes accompanying it.

Force governed by rage is not defensive force wearing an emotional costume. It is a different moral act, with different moral consequences, that the vocabulary of self-defense cannot legitimately claim.

Why Defensive Authority Ends When the Threat Ends

One of the clearest moral boundaries in the ethics of defensive force is this: defensive authority terminates when the threat that justified it ceases. Defense exists to stop harm. Once the harm is stopped, the justification grounding the defensive response has been fulfilled, and force continuing beyond that fulfillment is no longer defense in any morally meaningful sense.

This matters because the emotional conditions accompanying genuine defensive situations do not resolve the moment the threat is neutralized. Fear, adrenaline, and the residue of perceived violation do not switch off cleanly when physical danger passes.

The moral discipline required to cease force at the moment necessity ceases—to resist the emotional momentum toward punishment or retaliation—is precisely the discipline separating the morally serious defender from the person who began with a legitimate claim and allowed it to deteriorate into something else.

The excess that transforms a defender into an aggressor does not always announce itself dramatically. It can be a matter of degrees—force continuing slightly longer than necessity required, response escalating slightly beyond what the threat demanded.

The ethical burden does not diminish as force continues. It intensifies—and the moral standard becomes progressively more demanding as the situation moves further from the genuine necessity that initially grounded the response (Walzer, 1977).

Firearms and the Amplification of Responsibility

The particular characteristics of firearms—their range, speed, and the immediacy and severity of their consequences—amplify both the practical requirements of disciplined use and the moral stakes of undisciplined use.

Poor judgment with a firearm produces consequences that are typically irreversible and extend well beyond the immediate situation generating them.

This amplification does not argue against the defensive use of firearms. It argues for the seriousness with which that use must be prepared for, governed, and held accountable. Greater capability does not diminish moral responsibility.

It concentrates it, and the person who carries a firearm for defensive purposes carries with it an obligation to the quality of judgment that its use requires (Kleck, 1997). Training is not merely practical preparation for effective use. It is moral preparation for responsible use—the development of emotional regulation, situational judgment, and disciplined threat assessment that responsible response demands.

Moral Preparation, Humility, and the Ethics of Judgment

Why Defensive Decisions Occur Under Imperfect Conditions

Any moral framework for defensive force that does not account for the conditions under which defensive decisions are actually made has not engaged with the problem it claims to address. Defenders rarely possess certain information about the nature or severity of the threat. They rarely have time to deliberate with the care that calm moral reflection permits.

They operate under stress, fear, and uncertainty that systematically affect the quality of judgment in ways that neither good intentions nor prior training can entirely eliminate.

This is not an argument for moral permissiveness—for the conclusion that difficulty of defensive decisions exempts them from moral evaluation. It is an argument for moral realism—for recognition that the standard against which defensive decisions are measured must be calibrated to actual conditions under which human beings make them.

A moral framework evaluating decisions made under genuine threat by the standards available to a calm observer reviewing the situation afterward has not achieved greater ethical rigor. It has achieved a form of detachment from the human realities it was designed to address (Grossman, 1995).

Why Preparation Is a Moral Obligation

The recognition that defensive decisions occur under imperfect conditions does not reduce the obligation to prepare for them as thoroughly as possible. If anything, it intensifies it. The person who carries a firearm for defensive purposes without adequate preparation—physical, technical, psychological, and moral—has accepted the consequences of their capability without accepting the full scope of the responsibility that capability entails.

Preparation, properly understood, is not primarily technical. It is moral formation. It is the development, through sustained training and reflection, of the judgment, emotional regulation, and situational awareness that responsible defensive action requires—the cultivation, in advance of crisis, of the internal resources that the crisis itself will not provide time to develop.

A person who has prepared seriously is less likely to employ force unnecessarily, more capable of employing it effectively when necessary, and better equipped to recognize the boundaries that necessity and proportionality define (Robertson, 2019).

The Difference Between Defense and Vigilantism

The distinction between legitimate defense and vigilantism is not always obvious, partly because both can be superficially described as the use of force against those behaving wrongly. The moral difference lies almost entirely in purpose and restraint.

Defense seeks to interrupt immediate harm—to stop an unjust act currently in progress or immediately imminent, using the force genuinely required for that purpose. Vigilantism seeks something else: the punishment of perceived wrongdoing, the assertion of unilateral moral authority, the satisfaction of the belief that established systems of justice have failed and that private individuals must compensate through direct action unconstrained by necessity, proportionality, or legitimate authority.

The vigilante is not a defender operating under difficult circumstances. They are a person who has substituted their own judgment for that of a moral and legal order—not in a moment of genuine defensive necessity where no alternative existed, but as a considered choice to exercise punitive authority that no individual within a functioning moral framework legitimately possesses. The distinction lies primarily in what the force serves: the immediate protection of innocent life, or the imposition of personally determined consequences upon those judged to deserve them (Teichman, 1986).

Why Moral Humility Matters

Even the best-prepared, most seriously intentioned, most disciplined person exercising defensive force remains fallible. The person who carries defensive capability with the settled conviction that their judgment is reliable under all conditions—that their threat assessment is always accurate and their moral authority beyond question—has not achieved confidence. They have achieved a form of arrogance that the actual record of human error under pressure does not support.

Moral humility does not produce hesitation that disables effective response. It produces the seriousness that prevents casual resort to force and the self-examination that continues after force has been employed.

It is the recognition that conditional moral authority—exercised under conditions of genuine necessity, with acknowledgment that those conditions might be assessed incorrectly—is the only kind available to fallible human beings making irreversible decisions under genuine pressure. That recognition, maintained with discipline, is not a weakness in the moral framework of defense. It is one of its most important structural supports.

Thoughts to Ponder Boundaries That Preserve Moral Legitimacy

Proportionality and restraint are not constraints imposed reluctantly upon an otherwise unlimited right. They are the conditions without which the right of self-defense loses its moral content entirely. Defense without limits is not a more robust version of defense—it is something the moral tradition surrounding defensive force has consistently refused to protect, precisely because its protection would undermine the distinction between defender and aggressor that gives the entire framework its ethical coherence.

The legitimacy of self-defense depends not merely upon the presence of a genuine threat, but upon the disciplined governance of the response to that threat—shaped by necessity, bounded by proportionality, and sustained by the moral humility that acknowledges human fallibility without surrendering to it.

The chapters that follow shift attention toward the major religious traditions that have wrestled most seriously with these questions across centuries of sustained moral reflection—examining how Judaism, Christianity, Islam, Hinduism, Buddhism, and Sikhism each confronted the tension between compassion, justice, restraint, and the defense of innocent life.

The conversation begins with Judaism and the foundational principle anchoring every discussion that follows: the supreme obligation to preserve life.

PART III

Comparative Religious Perspectives on Self-Defense

(Chapters 8-13)

What does the Lord require of you but to do justice, to love mercy, and to walk humbly with your God? — Micah 6:8

Chapter 8:

Judaism and the Preservation of Life

Jewish ethics does not approach the question of self-defense through the comfortable distance of abstraction. It approaches it the way it approaches most moral questions—with unflinching attention to concrete human reality, the serious weight of obligation, and the recognition that moral reasoning untethered from practical consequence is not wisdom but evasion. The preservation of innocent life occupies the highest position in the Jewish moral hierarchy, and that elevation is not symbolic. It carries operational authority—shaping law, governing conduct, and generating obligations that extend far beyond personal preference.

What distinguishes the Jewish framework from other religious treatments of defensive force is its refusal of sentimentality in either direction. It does not romanticize violence. It does not romanticize passivity. It insists, with the clarity that only a tradition forged in proximity to genuine historical danger could produce, that the sanctity of life is not honored by permitting its destruction when protection was possible.

Pikuach Nefesh and the Supreme Value of Human Life

Understanding Pikuach Nefesh

The Hebrew principle of *pikuach nefesh*—the obligation to preserve human life—occupies a position in Jewish law that has no precise equivalent in most other moral traditions. It is not a general aspiration toward human welfare. It is a binding legal and moral obligation of the highest order, capable of overriding nearly every other commandment when the two come into conflict.

The practical implications are deliberately concrete. The Sabbath—one of the most sacred institutions in Jewish religious life—yields immediately and completely to *pikuach nefesh*. A person whose life is in danger may, and indeed must, violate Sabbath restrictions to secure their survival or the survival of another. The Talmud frames this not as a regrettable exception but as the expression of a moral priority so foundational that Sabbath observance would itself be diminished by allowing life to be lost in its name (Babylonian Talmud, Yoma 85b).

This hierarchy is philosophically significant. It establishes that within Jewish moral reasoning, the preservation of life is not merely one value among several to be weighed in a general calculus. It is the foundational value that gives other values their context and meaning.

Why Preservation Creates Obligation Rather Than Mere Permission

Many traditions acknowledge that defensive action may be permissible—that a person threatened with violence is not obligated to submit without response. Jewish ethics presses further: where innocent life can be protected and the capacity to protect it exists, moral duty emerges. Failure to act when action was possible is not neutrality. It is moral failure.

The rabbinic tradition developed this insight with characteristic precision. The principle that one may not stand idly by while another's life is endangered is not presented as advice or counsel of exceptional virtue. It is treated as a commandment carrying the same binding force as explicit moral requirements of Jewish law (Maimonides, *Mishneh Torah*, Laws of Murder 1:14).

This framing removes the comfort of regarding inaction as the safe ethical default. Within this framework, the person who possesses the capacity to protect innocent life and declines to exercise it has not achieved moral purity through restraint. They have committed a form of moral failure through abdication.

The Relationship Between Sacredness and Defensive Action

A surface reading of the commitment to the sanctity of life might suggest it argues against defensive force—that reverence for human life should produce reluctance to take it under any circumstances. Jewish moral logic runs in a different direction. If human life is genuinely sacred—possessing intrinsic worth that cannot be overridden by the aggression of another—then the protection of that life against unjust attack is not a compromise of its sanctity. It is one of the ways sanctity is honored in practice.

The theological philosopher David Novak argues that the Jewish commitment to human dignity generates a moral structure in which the defense of innocent life against unjust aggression is not merely tolerated but demanded by the very values that give the tradition its moral coherence (Novak, 1998).

To believe that human life is sacred is to accept that its destruction is a serious moral wrong—and to accept that is to accept an obligation toward preventing that wrong when prevention is possible.

Defense, within this framework, does not exist in tension with the sacredness of life. It exists in service to it.

Why Jewish Ethics Rejects Moral Neutrality in the Face of Harm

The Jewish moral tradition has consistently resisted treating inaction as automatically innocent—regarding the person who stands by while harm occurs as morally clean by virtue of having kept their own hands free. Moral responsibility is not discharged by the mere absence of personal participation in harm. Where harm was foreseeable, capacity to interrupt it existed, and intervention was not itself prohibited by overriding considerations, the failure to intervene carries moral weight that cannot be dissolved by pointing to the absence of direct action.

Scriptural and Rabbinic Foundations for Self-Defense

Exodus and the Recognition of Imminent Threat

The Hebrew Bible addresses defensive force with a directness that distinguishes it from more ambiguous treatments elsewhere in ancient religious literature.

The passage in Exodus 22:2–3 concerning the lawful killing of a nighttime intruder establishes a foundational principle that rabbinic reasoning would develop across centuries: that the perception of imminent lethal threat creates a condition in which defensive killing is morally justified (Exodus 22:2–3). The rabbinic analysis of this passage is instructive not merely for its conclusion but for its method:

The sages did not treat the text as a blanket permission for violence against any intruder under any circumstances. They examined it with careful attention to context, intention, and moral asymmetry. The nighttime intruder was presumed dangerous because the combination of darkness, trespass, and reasonable assumption of violent intent created a moral situation in which the defender could not be expected to assume otherwise.

The analysis turns on moral probability—on what a reasonable person, confronting the available information in real time, could conclude about the nature of the threat they faced. This approach reflects a legal tradition deeply committed to the practical realities of human moral experience rather than its idealized abstractions.

"Do Not Stand Idly By the Blood of Your Neighbor"

The commandment recorded in Leviticus 19:16—*lo ta'amod al dam re'echa*, typically rendered as "do not stand idly by the blood of your neighbor"—is among the most direct statements of defensive obligation in any religious tradition (Leviticus 19:16).

Its interpretation within the rabbinic tradition extends beyond the prohibition of passive witnessing to establish a positive obligation of intervention—a duty to take active steps to prevent harm to others when such steps are available.

The moral philosopher and Talmudic scholar Aharon Lichtenstein argued that this commandment represents one of Judaism's most characteristic moral insights: that ethical life is not merely the management of one's own conduct but the active exercise of responsibility toward others whose welfare lies within one's sphere of influence (Lichtenstein, 2004). This framing transforms the defense of others from a morally praiseworthy choice that exceeds ordinary obligation into an expectation that ordinary moral seriousness generates.

Rabbinic Teachings on Defensive Necessity

The Talmudic principle *ha-ba le-horgecha, hashkem le-horgo*—"if someone comes to kill you, rise early and kill him first"—is among the most direct statements of defensive preemption in the Jewish legal tradition (Babylonian Talmud, Sanhedrin 72a). Its moral logic is precise. The principle does not license aggression toward those who have expressed hostility at some future time. It addresses the specific moral situation of a person confronting an aggressor whose lethal intent is clear and whose capacity to execute that intent is imminent.

The framing is stated not as a permission reluctantly extended but as an imperative—an instruction to act rather than wait. The moral reasoning reflects the tradition's consistent position that the innocent person facing a lethal threat is not obligated to accept passive annihilation. The aggressor, by initiating the lethal confrontation, has created a moral situation in which the defender's action is not merely permitted but required by the same principles governing the obligation to preserve innocent life. This must be understood within proper moral boundaries: the principle concerns a genuine, imminent, lethal threat—not anticipatory aggression based on speculation about future harm.

Why Jewish Law Simultaneously Affirms Defense and Restraint

The most important feature of the Jewish ethical framework for defensive force is not its affirmation of self-defense but its insistence that affirmation and restraint are expressions of the same underlying moral commitment. The *pikuach nefesh* principle that grounds the obligation to preserve life does not distinguish, in its fundamental logic, between the life of the innocent victim and the life of the aggressor. Both are human lives. The justification for defensive force rests not upon the claim that the aggressor's life is worthless—it rests upon the claim that the aggressor's choices have created a moral situation in which the only available means of preserving innocent life also places the aggressor's life at risk.

This means that moral permission to employ defensive force terminates with the threat that generated it. Once the aggressor no longer poses imminent danger, the justification grounded in necessity no longer applies. Force continuing beyond this point is not the continuation of legitimate defense.

It is retaliation, which the tradition treats as a categorically different and significantly less defensible moral act (Maimonides, *Mishneh Torah*, Laws of Murder 1:6–7). The discipline required to recognize and honor this boundary—to cease force at the moment necessity ceases rather than when anger subsides—is precisely the discipline that Jewish legal reasoning builds into its treatment of defensive obligation.

Preparedness, Defensive Capability, and Moral Responsibility

Why Defensive Capability Matters Morally

A moral obligation to preserve life is not discharged by the sincerity of intention to protect. It requires practical capacity to make protection effective. The tradition's insistence that *pikuach nefesh* generates genuine obligation rather than mere aspiration has direct implications for preparedness: a person who accepts the moral duty to protect innocent life must also accept responsibility for ensuring their capacity to do so is adequate to the threats they may actually face. This connection between obligation and capability reflects the tradition's characteristic insistence on the practical dimensions of moral responsibility—its refusal to accept a form of moral seriousness that expresses itself in intention alone while remaining indifferent to whether the outcomes it values are actually secured (Novak, 1998).

The right to self-defense, understood within *pikuach nefesh*, is not primarily a personal prerogative. It is part of the broader obligation of moral agents to take seriously the protection of human life—an obligation extending to ensuring that the means of that protection are genuine and effective.

Historical Jewish Experience and the Reality of Vulnerability

The Jewish ethical tradition did not develop its understanding of defensive obligation in the comfort of sustained security. It developed across centuries of recurring persecution, displacement, and violence—in communities that understood, from repeated painful experience, the difference between moral reasoning adequate to protected existence and moral reasoning adequate to genuine vulnerability (Johnson, 1987).

This context does not determine the content of the tradition's moral conclusions, but it explains their character: the directness with which they engage the reality of threat, the practical seriousness with which they treat the obligation to protect, and the absence of comfortable abstraction that tends to characterize ethical reasoning produced at a safe distance from the dangers it addresses.

The tradition of communal defense—the recognition that responsibility for the protection of the vulnerable extends beyond the individual to the community—reflects this historical experience with particular clarity. Jewish legal and ethical reasoning consistently emphasized shared responsibility for the security of those who could not protect themselves, treating the defense of the community's vulnerable members as an expression of the same obligations governing individual self-defense.

Why Judaism Rejects the Idea That Virtue Equals Helplessness

The suggestion that moral virtue is expressed through cultivated incapacity finds no support in the Jewish ethical tradition. Within the framework of *pikuach nefesh*, strength used in the disciplined protection of innocent life is not a moral compromise. It is the expression of a moral commitment in the form that the situation demands.

The distinction the tradition draws is not between strength and weakness but between strength governed by moral purpose and strength exercised for domination, revenge, or ego. Weakness that permits injustice to proceed unchallenged is not morally superior to disciplined strength that prevents itand the tradition's sustained insistence upon the obligation to protect innocent life makes this conclusion not merely permissible but necessary.

Firearms Within the Framework of Jewish Moral Reasoning

Jewish moral reasoning does not evaluate instruments in isolation from their use. A firearm, within the framework of *pikuach nefesh*, is evaluated according to the same criteria applied to every other dimension of defensive capacity: does its possession and use serve the preservation of innocent life? Is it governed by necessity and proportionality?

Does it remain subject to the moral boundaries the tradition insists upon—the termination of force when the threat ceases, the restraint distinguishing protection from retaliation, the accountability that moral seriousness requires?

These questions do not produce a simple categorical answer about any particular instrument. They produce a framework within which specific instances of defensive capability can be evaluated with the seriousness and contextual attention that the Jewish legal tradition brings to moral questions generally. The central ethical question is not whether force exists but whether it serves preservation rather than oppression—and whether the person exercising it has accepted, along with the capability, the full weight of the moral responsibility that capability generates (Telushkin, 1994).

Thoughts to Ponder: Life Above All

Judaism offers one of the most direct and philosophically serious religious affirmations of the duty to preserve innocent life available in any major moral tradition. *Pikuach nefesh* places that duty at the apex of the moral hierarchy, generating obligations that extend from the individual to the community and from intention to practical capacity. The tradition does not glorify violence. It recognizes, with the honesty that a history of genuine vulnerability produces, that sacred life sometimes requires courageous protection—and that the moral failure to provide that protection when it was possible is not innocence. It is a different kind of wrong.

Defensive force, within the Jewish framework, is morally legitimate when necessary, proportionate, and directed at preservation rather than retaliation. These conditions are demanding. They are meant to be. The seriousness of the obligation to preserve life is matched, within the tradition, by the seriousness of the constraints governing how that preservation may be pursued.

The next chapter turns to Christianity—a tradition that inherited significant elements of this framework while developing its own complex engagement with the tension between love, justice, sacrifice, and the question of when, if ever, the follower of a gospel of peace may take up the sword.

Chapter 9:

Christianity—Love, Justice, and the Sword

Few traditions have been more consistently misrepresented in modern discussions of defensive ethics than Christianity. The popular caricature presents a faith requiring total non-resistance—a religion whose ethics reduce, in practice, to the selective application of a handful of phrases stripped of their historical and textual contexts. This caricature serves the convenience of argument. It does not survive serious engagement with the tradition itself.

Christianity is neither militaristic nor absolutely pacifist. It is something considerably more demanding than either: a moral framework that holds love and justice together without collapsing one into the other, that takes seriously both the command to love one's neighbor and the concrete reality of what that neighbor's safety sometimes requires, and that has wrestled for two thousand years with the tension between the imperative of peace and the reality of predatory evil.

Love, Human Dignity, and the Moral Duty to Protect

The Christian Understanding of Human Worth

The foundation of Christian ethics is not a code of conduct but a claim about the nature of human beings—that every person, regardless of circumstance or capacity, bears the image of God and therefore possesses inherent dignity that cannot be legitimately overridden. This theological conviction is not incidental to Christian moral reasoning. It is the premise from which its ethical structure follows.

The practical implications extend directly into defensive ethics. If every human life possesses sacred worth—worth not contingent upon power or the willingness of the powerful to respect it—then the destruction of innocent life at the hands of an aggressor represents a moral wrong of the highest order.

And if it represents a genuine moral wrong, then preventing it, including through necessary and proportionate force, is not a peripheral ethical concern. It is a direct expression of the same commitment to human dignity from which the command to love one's neighbor derives its content (Lewis, 1952).

The command to love one's neighbor is not a sentimental instruction to feel warmly toward those nearby. It presupposes active concern for that neighbor's continued safety and existence. A love that remains indifferent to the destruction of the beloved is not love in any morally serious sense. It is an emotional preference unconnected to moral responsibility.

Why Love Is More Than Passive Sentiment

Christian love—*agape* in the Greek of the New Testament—is consistently presented not as a feeling but as a commitment expressed through action. It moves toward the wounded traveler rather than passing on the other side of the road. It is, at its most demanding, the love that places the welfare of another above the comfort of the one who loves. The theologian Dietrich Bonhoeffer, whose moral reasoning was tested under conditions few thinkers ever face, concluded that responsible action sometimes requires accepting the burden of difficult choices rather than retreating into the purity of non-involvement. Writing from within Nazi Germany, Bonhoeffer argued that the person who refuses to engage with genuine evil in order to preserve their own moral cleanliness has not achieved virtue—they have achieved a form of irresponsibility that wears virtue's clothing (Bonhoeffer, 1955).

Love that refuses to confront preventable destruction sacrifices the beloved to the comfort of the one who loves.

"Turn the Other Cheek" and the Context of Personal Insult

No passage is more frequently invoked in discussions of Christian ethics and violence than Christ's instruction to turn the other cheek—and few are more consistently misread.

The instruction occurs within a specific moral context: the response to personal insult, social humiliation, and ego-driven retaliation. It addresses the internal disposition of the believer toward their own mistreatment—the cultivation of humility over pride, forgiveness over vengeance.

What it does not address is the situation of a person confronting a lethal threat to themselves or others. The theologian N.T. Wright argues that Christ's teaching here is directed at the transformation of personal moral character—the refusal to be defined by one's injuries—rather than at the establishment of universal non-resistance applicable to every circumstance involving force (Wright, 2004).

Christianity condemns retaliatory hatred and ego-driven violence. It has not, in its mainstream moral tradition, condemned the morally restrained protection of innocent life.

Why Christianity Distinguishes Between Revenge and Defense

The distinction between revenge and defense is embedded in Christianity's most fundamental moral categories. Revenge looks backward—responding to prior injury, seeking satisfaction for a grievance. Defense looks forward—responding to present threat, seeking interruption of ongoing harm oriented toward preservation rather than punishment.

This distinction maps directly onto the Christian distinction between sins of pride—of which revenge is paradigmatically one—and the obligations of love and duty requiring active engagement with the world's dangers. The person employing force to protect an innocent life at genuine risk is not acting from the same moral impulse as the person satisfying wounded pride. The Christian moral tradition has consistently recognized this difference and evaluated the two acts accordingly.

Justice, Authority, and the Moral Reality of Force

The Sword as Symbol of Restrained Justice

Paul's treatment of governing authority in Romans 13 is among the most significant passages in the Christian tradition for the ethics of force. The governing authority, Paul argues, does not bear the sword in vain—it exists as the servant of God for the restraint of wrongdoing and the protection of those who do right (Romans 13:1–4). This is not a glorification of violence. It is an acknowledgment that justice, to be effective rather than merely aspirational, requires the capacity for enforcement—and that enforcement, in a world containing genuine predatory evil, cannot be entirely non-coercive. Paul's framing presents the restraint of wrongdoing as a genuine moral function serving the protection of the innocent. Force exercised in this service is not portrayed as a regrettable concession to human sinfulness. It is presented as a dimension of the moral order established for the governance of human communities in a world that contains real evil.

Christ's Teachings on Preparedness and Prudence

The Gospel accounts contain passages that sit uncomfortably alongside the popular image of Christianity as requiring passive non-resistance. In Luke 22:36, Christ instructs his disciples—in circumstances of genuine danger—that those without a sword should sell their cloaks to acquire one (Luke 22:36). Its existence in the text represents an acknowledgment of vulnerability and an instruction toward practical preparedness that cannot be reconciled with the claim that Christian ethics uniformly prohibits defensive readiness.

More broadly, the imagery of the good shepherd who defends the flock against the wolf—in contrast to the hired hand who abandons the sheep when danger arrives—presents protective readiness as virtue rather than moral failure (John 10:11–13). Trust in God, within the Christian framework, does not eliminate the responsibility of practical stewardship toward those in one's care.

Augustine, Aquinas, and the Just War Tradition

The most sustained Christian engagement with the ethics of force is the just war tradition, developed from Augustine's early formulations through Aquinas's systematic treatment into the body of moral theology that continues to influence both religious and secular discussions of legitimate force today. Augustine argued that force could be morally legitimate when directed toward the restraint of evil and the protection of the innocent—but that its moral character depended entirely upon the interior disposition of those who employed it.

Force motivated by love of the neighbor's safety and governed by the intention to restore peace was categorically different from force motivated by hatred or domination (Augustine, trans. 1984). The difference was not primarily in the external act but in the moral agent performing it.

Aquinas systematized this insight into explicit criteria shaping Western moral and legal thinking ever since: just cause, right intention, legitimate authority, last resort, probability of success, and proportionate means (Aquinas, c. 1265–1274).

These criteria were not designed to make the use of force easy. They were designed to ensure that force, when employed, remained within the moral boundaries that could justify it—maintaining the tradition's commitment to peace as the ultimate goal even within its acknowledgment that peace sometimes requires defense.

Why Christianity Rejects Both Brutality and Passive Indifference

The Christian tradition has found itself in genuine tension with two mirror-image failures: the failure of brutality, in which force is employed without adequate moral constraint in the service of pride or domination; and the failure of passive indifference, in which the innocent are abandoned to preventable harm in the name of a purity that costs nothing and accomplishes less.

The theologian Reinhold Niebuhr argued that the refusal to employ force in defense of the innocent—when such refusal permits preventable injustice—reflects not moral elevation but a form of irresponsibility the tradition's own commitments cannot sustain (Niebuhr, 1932). Love and justice are not opposites within the Christian framework. Justice is the structural form that love takes when it must operate in a world containing genuine predatory evil—and the willingness to enforce just boundaries, at real personal cost, is among the most demanding expressions of love the tradition recognizes.

Stewardship, Restraint, and the Moral Burden of Defense

Why Defense Is a Burden Rather Than a Fantasy

Christianity does not present the use of defensive force as a triumph. It presents it as a burden—one that may be morally necessary but carries emotional, psychological, and spiritual weight the serious Christian does not expect to escape simply because their cause is just. The tradition's insistence on the moral seriousness of taking human life, even in legitimate defense, reflects its conviction that every human life possesses sacred worth—including the life of the aggressor whose choices created the situation requiring defensive force.

Grief in the aftermath of defensive action is not evidence of moral failure. It is evidence of moral seriousness—recognition that something of genuine value has been lost, even when the loss was unavoidable. Bonhoeffer's concept of responsible action captures this precisely: The morally serious person accepts the burden of difficult choices in the world as it actually is, bears the weight of their consequences, and does not expect the difficulty of the choice to dissolve simply because the choice was right (Bonhoeffer, 1955).

Firearms as Instruments of Stewardship Rather Than Domination

The Christian evaluation of any instrument of defensive force is directed not at the instrument itself but at the moral agent who employs it and the purposes that employment serves. A firearm, within Christian moral reasoning, possesses no independent moral status. Its ethical character derives entirely from the intention, restraint, necessity, and accountability of the person who bears it.

The concept of stewardship—the Christian understanding that human beings are entrusted with capabilities they are responsible to use well—provides the most useful framework for approaching defensive capability. The steward holds capability in trust, with responsibility for how it is exercised, toward ends transcending personal preferences or emotional states.

Applied to defensive capacity, this framework generates the same requirements that appear throughout the tradition's treatment of force: last-resort thinking, proportionate response, protective rather than punitive purpose, and the accountability of conscience before and after action is taken.

The Problem of Delegated Moral Responsibility

Christian moral reasoning does not permit the comfortable evasion of responsibility through institutional delegation. The person who declines all personal engagement with the ethics of defensive force while depending upon police and armed citizens to confront violence on their behalf has not achieved moral consistency. They have achieved moral outsourcing—the transfer of an uncomfortable burden to others while claiming the benefits of the protection that burden provides. This is not an argument against institutional structures of protection. It is an argument for honesty about what those structures involve.

The officer who places themselves between the public and violence bears a moral burden that does not disappear because it has been institutionalized. And the person whose safety depends upon their willingness cannot claim moral superiority through the simple expedient of declining to share it.

Humility, Strength, and Moral Self-Command

The Christian tradition praises humility—but humility, properly understood, is not the same as cultivated helplessness. Humility concerns the proper ordering of the self in relation to God and others—the refusal to place personal pride or the desire for domination at the center of moral decision-making. It has nothing inherently to say against the possession and disciplined exercise of capability in the service of genuine love and protection.

C.S. Lewis observed that the ideal the Christian tradition actually commends is not the person incapable of strength but the person who possesses strength and has brought it under the governance of conscience and love—who could act from pride and chooses not to, who could employ force beyond what necessity requires and restrains themselves, and who serves rather than dominates (Lewis, 1952).

The Christian ideal is disciplined strength governed by love—and love, as the tradition insists, is not a feeling. It is a commitment expressed through action, including the difficult action of standing between the innocent and those who would harm them.

Thoughts to Ponder: Love Strong Enough to Protect

Christianity does not require the surrender of innocent life to evil in the name of moral purity. Its most serious moral thinkers—from Augustine through Aquinas to Bonhoeffer and Niebuhr—have consistently recognized that love and justice are not opposites, that force governed by conscience can serve genuinely moral purposes, and that the refusal to engage with the ethics of defense is not spiritual elevation but moral incompleteness.

The Christian who bears defensive capability seriously—governed by humility rather than pride, by necessity rather than aggression, and by the sorrow appropriate to the weight of what they carry—is not departing from the tradition's moral vision. They are expressing one of its most demanding dimensions: the willingness to accept the burden of responsible action in a world containing genuine evil, without becoming, in the process, what they sought to resist.

Christian love does not require passivity in the face of injustice. It requires the moral courage to resist injustice without becoming unjust—and the discipline, conscience, and humility to maintain that distinction under pressure.

The next chapter turns to Islam—a tradition whose treatment of defensive force, restraint, and the protection of innocent life is as carefully developed and as frequently misunderstood as Christianity's own.

Chapter 10:

Islam—Defense, Restraint, and the Protection of the Innocent

Few traditions suffer more consistently from the substitution of political caricature for serious moral engagement than Islam.

Modern discourse about Islamic ethics and violence tends to filter the tradition through the lens of contemporary conflict rather than through the classical scholarship, legal reasoning, and theological reflection that actually constitute its moral framework.

The result is a distorted picture—one that either exaggerates Islam's relationship to violence or, in overcorrection, denies the tradition's serious and sophisticated engagement with the ethics of defensive force altogether.

Islamic ethics neither glorifies violence nor denies the reality of injustice.

It approaches force the way it approaches most serious moral questions—with careful attention to intention, necessity, accountability, and the weight of consequences before God.

Defense is treated not as a celebration of power but as a constrained moral response to injustice already in motion, bounded by principles that have been developed with considerable precision across fourteen centuries of jurisprudential and theological reflection.

The Sanctity of Life and the Moral Legitimacy of Defense

The Sacredness of Human Life in Islamic Moral Thought

The Islamic moral framework begins with a conviction about human life that shapes everything built upon it: life is not a human possession to be disposed of according to preference or circumstance. It is a trust, an *amanah*—held from God, carrying inherent dignity that cannot be legitimately violated without the gravest moral consequence. The Qur'an expresses this with striking directness: the unjust killing of a single soul is treated as equivalent in gravity to the killing of all humanity, and the preservation of a single soul as equivalent to the preservation of all (Qur'an 5:32).

This foundational conviction produces a moral framework in which force is not a casual instrument. The taking of human life—even the life of an aggressor under conditions of genuine defensive necessity—carries weight that the tradition does not allow to be minimized or celebrated. The moral seriousness with which Islamic ethics treats life is precisely what shapes the moral seriousness with which it approaches every situation in which life may be threatened or taken.

The classical scholars of Islamic jurisprudence—the *fuqaha*—developed from this foundation an elaborate framework of moral and legal reasoning governing the conditions under which force might be employed, the limitations that must constrain it, and the accountability that must follow it. This framework is not peripheral to Islamic moral thought. It is one of its most carefully developed domains.

Qur'anic Permission for Defense Against Injustice

The Qur'an's treatment of defensive force is direct and its moral logic clear. Permission to resist aggression is explicitly granted to those who have been wronged—to those attacked, expelled unjustly from their homes, oppressed, or threatened with harm they have done nothing to deserve. The Qur'an frames this permission in terms of the moral asymmetry between the aggressor and the defender: the aggressor has initiated the injustice, bears the responsibility for its escalation, and cannot claim the protections that attach to those who have not chosen violence (Qur'an 22:39–40).

This framing reflects the same moral insight that appears across the traditions examined in preceding chapters: that defensive force is reactive rather than initiatory, that its moral character derives from its relationship to injustice already in motion, and that the defender occupies a fundamentally different moral position from the aggressor who created the situation requiring response.

The Qur'anic permission for defense is not a license for aggression dressed in defensive vocabulary. It is a recognition that the person facing genuine unjust harm has a morally legitimate claim to resist it—and that resistance, under the conditions and within the limitations the tradition specifies, honors rather than violates the sanctity of life that Islamic ethics places at its center.

Why Defense Is Not Viewed as Moral Corruption

A recurring concern in religious traditions that place high value on human life and peace is whether the permission to employ defensive force represents a compromise of those values—a pragmatic concession to human sinfulness that sits uneasily alongside the tradition's higher aspirations. Islamic moral reasoning addresses this concern directly and without apology. Defense, within the framework of Islamic ethics, is not a compromise of the commitment to the sanctity of life. It is an expression of it.

The moral philosopher Seyyed Hossein Nasr, in his examination of Islamic ethics, argues that the tradition's permission for defensive force reflects its honest engagement with the world as it actually is—a world in which injustice is real, in which the innocent are genuinely vulnerable, and in which the refusal to acknowledge this reality produces not moral elevation but moral negligence (Nasr, 2003). Force used to preserve innocent life against genuine threat differs morally from force used to dominate, intimidate, or punish—and the Islamic tradition's sophisticated jurisprudential framework exists precisely to maintain and enforce this distinction.

Why Passivity in the Face of Preventable Harm Is Morally Problematic

Islamic ethics does not treat inaction in the face of preventable harm as automatically virtuous. The tradition's emphasis on moral responsibility—on the accountability of each person before God for the choices they make and the consequences those choices produce—extends to the consequences of chosen inaction as surely as it extends to the consequences of action. Where the capacity to protect exists, and where genuine threat to innocent life is present, the failure to employ that capacity carries moral weight that cannot be discharged by the mere absence of personal involvement in harm.

This moral structure reflects the broader Islamic understanding of *khalifah*—the human being's role as steward of creation, bearing responsibility not merely for their own conduct but for the welfare of those within their sphere of influence and capability (Kamali, 2008). The parent, the community member, the person capable of intervention who stands by while preventable harm occurs has not preserved their moral purity. They have failed a moral obligation whose seriousness the tradition treats with the same gravity it applies to active wrongdoing.

Restraint, Proportionality, and Moral Accountability

The Qur'anic Prohibition Against Transgression

The Qur'anic framework governing defensive force is structured by a principle of striking moral precision: permission to resist aggression is granted, but transgression—*'udwan*—is simultaneously and explicitly prohibited. The Qur'an's instruction is direct: fight in the way of God against those who fight you, but do not transgress, for God does not love transgressors (Qur'an 2:190). This formulation is not a footnote attached reluctantly to the permission for defense. It is the moral architecture within which that permission exists and outside which it ceases to be morally legitimate.

The prohibition against transgression establishes that victory alone does not determine moral legitimacy. The manner in which force is employed, the degree to which it remains within the boundaries of genuine defensive necessity, and the intention governing it—these are the criteria by which Islamic ethics evaluates the moral character of defensive action. An act that begins as legitimate defense and extends into excess, cruelty, or punishment beyond what necessity required has not remained within the moral space the tradition's permission occupies.

It has crossed into transgression—and transgression, regardless of how it began, is condemned with the same moral seriousness as the aggression it originally sought to resist.

Islamic Jurisprudence and Defensive Limitation

The classical scholars of Islamic jurisprudence developed a framework for governing defensive force that is remarkable for its precision and its sustained commitment to moral limitation.

Drawing upon Qur'anic principles, the traditions of the Prophet (*hadith*), and centuries of careful legal reasoning, the *fuqaha* established conditions that must be met for defensive force to retain its moral legitimacy across the full duration of its exercise.

Imminence requires that the threat be present and immediate rather than speculative or remote. Necessity demands that defensive force be employed only when no less harmful alternative is genuinely available. Proportionality insists that the response bear a reasonable relationship to the threat, not exceeding what genuine defensive purpose requires.

And the termination principle holds that the moral permission for defensive force ceases at the moment the threat ceases—that force continuing beyond the cessation of danger has converted itself from defense into retaliation, which the tradition evaluates under an entirely different and significantly stricter moral standard (Ibn Rushd, trans. 1994).

These conditions were not developed as academic exercises in legal theory. They were developed as practical moral boundaries designed to ensure that the permission for defensive force did not expand, through the rationalizations that accompany conflict, into a general license for violence that the tradition had never intended to grant.

Why Intention Matters in Islamic Ethics

The Islamic ethical tradition places unusual emphasis on intention—*niyyah*—as a determinant of the moral character of action. The Prophet's famous statement that actions are judged by intentions, and that each person will receive what they intended, is not merely a pious observation. It is a foundational principle of Islamic moral and legal reasoning that applies with particular force in the domain of defensive action (Bukhari, Sahih al-Bukhari, Book 1, Hadith 1).

This emphasis on intention does not diminish the importance of the act itself or its consequences. It adds a dimension of moral evaluation that consequences alone cannot capture. Defensive force motivated by genuine concern for the preservation of innocent life—by the responsibility to protect those who cannot protect themselves, by the obligation to interrupt injustice rather than to satisfy grievance—occupies a different moral category from force motivated by revenge, pride, the desire for domination, or the emotional satisfaction of answered injury. The outward act may appear identical. The moral reality, within the Islamic framework, is not.

This insistence on the moral significance of intention is among the reasons that Islamic ethics is so resistant to the mechanical application of rules divorced from context. The tradition does not simply ask what was done. It asks why—and it holds the person accountable to the honesty of their own answer before God.

Why Islamic Ethics Rejects Both Brutality and Helplessness

The moral ideal that emerges from the Islamic tradition's engagement with defensive force is neither the person incapable of effective response nor the person who employs force without restraint or moral accountability. It is the person who possesses genuine capability and governs it with the discipline, intention, and conscience that the tradition demands—who resists injustice without becoming unjust, who employs force when genuine necessity requires it and restrains themselves the moment necessity ceases, and who bears the weight of their choices with the humility and accountability that standing before God requires.

The scholar Tariq Ramadan, in his examination of Islamic ethics in the contemporary world, argues that the tradition's moral framework consistently refuses both the false comfort of helplessness and the moral corruption of unrestrained force—insisting instead upon the difficult middle ground of disciplined responsibility that genuine moral seriousness requires (Ramadan, 2009).

Strength governed .by justice is not corruption in the Islamic framework. Weakness that permits injustice to proceed unchallenged is not virtue. The moral terrain the tradition occupies lies between these failures, and navigating it requires the formation of character that the tradition's ethical and spiritual disciplines are designed to produce.

Preparedness, Responsibility, and the Protection of the Innocent

Why Protection of the Innocent Is Central in Islamic Ethics

The obligation to protect the vulnerable—children, families, the defenseless, and communities facing genuine threat—is not peripheral to Islamic moral reasoning.

It flows directly from the tradition's foundational conviction about the sanctity of human life and the stewardship responsibilities that conviction generates. The *maqasid al-shariah*—the objectives of Islamic law as identified by classical scholars—place the preservation of life, mind, lineage, and property among the highest purposes that the tradition's legal and ethical framework exists to serve (Al-Ghazali, trans. 2013).

This framework means that the protection of innocent life is not merely permitted within Islamic ethics. Under conditions of genuine threat and available capability, it rises to the level of obligation—a moral duty whose seriousness is proportional to the seriousness with which the tradition treats the lives it seeks to protect. The person who possesses the capacity to protect innocent life and declines to exercise it when genuine threat is present has not preserved their moral purity. They have failed a responsibility that the tradition's own foundational commitments generate.

Defensive Responsibility Beyond Institutions

Islamic ethics values governance and legal authority. The tradition's emphasis on social order, communal welfare, and the proper functioning of institutions that protect and regulate human communities reflects a genuine conviction that organized social life is among the conditions under which human beings can fulfill their moral and spiritual potential. The scholar of Islamic law Mohammad Hashim Kamali notes that Islamic jurisprudence consistently treats the maintenance of social order as a foundational moral obligation whose importance extends to every member of the community (Kamali, 2008).

But the tradition's emphasis on institutional structures does not dissolve individual moral responsibility when those structures are unavailable, inadequate, or absent.

The moral obligation to protect innocent life—grounded in *pikuach nefesh*'s Islamic equivalent, the *maqasid*'s preservation of life—belongs to the individual moral agent as well as to the collective.

When institutional protection fails to materialize in time, when circumstances place individuals in situations where no institutional response is available, the underlying moral responsibility to preserve innocent life remains. It has not been transferred to an institution that has not appeared. It rests, as it always has, with the person present and capable.

Firearms Within the Islamic Ethical Framework

Islamic moral reasoning does not treat the specific instruments of defensive force as morally significant in themselves. A firearm, within the framework of Islamic ethics, is evaluated by the same criteria applied to every other dimension of defensive capability: does its possession and use serve the preservation of innocent life? Is it governed by the necessity, proportionality, and restraint that the tradition demands? Does it remain subject to the moral boundaries that distinguish legitimate defense from transgression?

These questions do not produce categorical condemnation of any particular instrument of defense. They produce a framework within which defensive capability—including firearms—can be evaluated according to the moral standards that the tradition brings to every practical question involving force. What matters, within this framework, is not the nature of the tool but the character, intention, and accountability of the person who employs it. The central ethical question is whether the capability serves justice within the limitations that Islamic moral reasoning requires—and whether the person bearing it has accepted, along with the capability, the full weight of the moral responsibility that capability generates before God.

Humility, Reflection, and the Moral Weight of Defensive Force

The Islamic tradition does not permit the use of defensive force to be morally casual. Even where necessity clearly justifies action, even where proportionality is maintained and transgression avoided, the taking of human life carries spiritual and emotional weight that the tradition insists upon acknowledging. The classical scholars consistently emphasized that the person who employs defensive force—even force that is fully justified by the conditions the tradition specifies—must approach that experience with humility, reflection, and the accountability that standing before God requires.

This insistence reflects the tradition's deepest conviction about the relationship between human moral agency and divine accountability. The person who employs force without subsequent reflection—who treats the exercise of defensive capability as an occasion for pride rather than an occasion for the sober acknowledgment of what human violence costs—has missed what the tradition regards as among the most important moral lessons that genuine defensive necessity can teach. The weight of what occurred, even when it was right, is itself a form of moral education. And the humility that weight produces is among the most important qualities that the tradition seeks to cultivate in those who bear defensive responsibility.

Thoughts to Ponder: Justice Under Restraint

Islamic ethics offers a framework for defensive force that is simultaneously serious and carefully bounded—one that affirms the moral legitimacy of resistance to injustice while insisting upon the restraint, accountability, and humility that legitimate resistance requires. Human life is sacred. Its destruction is among the gravest moral wrongs the tradition recognizes. And it is precisely because life is sacred that its protection, under conditions of genuine necessity and within the limits that moral accountability demands, rises to the level of obligation rather than remaining merely a personal option.

The tradition does not glorify force. It recognizes that justice sometimes requires disciplined resistance to injustice—resistance governed not by pride, hatred, or the desire for domination but by the sober acceptance of moral responsibility before both the human community and God. That recognition, expressed across fourteen centuries of careful jurisprudential and theological reasoning, places Islamic ethics squarely within the convergence of moral traditions this book has traced—traditions that differ in their specific formulations but agree in their foundational insistence that force, when genuinely necessary, must remain the servant of conscience rather than its replacement.

The next chapter turns to Hinduism—a tradition whose engagement with the ethics of duty, moral conflict, and righteous defense reaches its most searching expression in one of the world's most philosophically sophisticated sacred texts.

Chapter 11:

Hinduism—Dharma, Duty, and Righteous Defense

Hindu moral philosophy does not ask simply whether force is good or evil. It asks something more demanding: what does righteousness require under these specific conditions, given this person's role, capacity, and obligation within the moral order? This is the question that *dharma*—the central organizing principle of Hindu ethics—places at the heart of every serious moral decision. Dharma is not a fixed code applied uniformly to every situation. It is the discernment of right action within the full complexity of circumstance, role, and responsibility. It does not offer the comfort of simple rules. It demands the harder work of honest moral reasoning under genuine pressure.

The Bhagavad Gita—the philosophical dialogue embedded within the epic Mahabharata—remains the most searching exploration of this demand in the Hindu tradition. It begins not in peace but in crisis, and its moral authority derives precisely from its refusal to resolve that crisis cheaply.

Arjuna's Crisis and the Moral Weight of Duty

The Battlefield Setting of the Bhagavad Gita

The Bhagavad Gita opens on a battlefield where two armies have assembled for a conflict that will determine the fate of a kingdom. At the center of this scene stands Arjuna—a warrior of exceptional capability, facing opponents who include his own teachers, kinsmen, and friends. Confronting this reality, Arjuna's bow falls from his hands. He cannot bring himself to fight. The prospect of violence against those he loves overwhelms him, and he collapses into what the text presents not as cowardice but as a genuine moral crisis—the experience of a person who takes seriously what violence costs and who finds that seriousness temporarily paralyzing (Bhagavad Gita 1:28–47).

The Gita's moral authority begins here. It does not dismiss Arjuna's anguish. It does not treat his compassion as a weakness to be overcome or his grief as an obstacle to be cleared away. It takes seriously the emotional and moral weight of what he faces—and then, through the dialogue between Arjuna and Krishna that constitutes the text's philosophical substance, it examines whether his response to that weight reflects genuine moral wisdom or a form of avoidance wearing wisdom's clothing.

Arjuna's Desire to Withdraw From Conflict

Arjuna's position has the appearance of moral seriousness. He does not want to kill. He does not desire the victory that the conflict would bring. He is willing to accept loss, displacement, and even death rather than participate in violence against people he loves. From the perspective of many moral traditions, this willingness to absorb harm rather than inflict it might seem like the highest expression of moral commitment.

Krishna's response in the Gita challenges this reading—not by dismissing the compassion from which it springs but by examining what it actually produces. The philosopher Jonardon Ganeri, in his study of Indian moral philosophy, notes that the Gita's critique of Arjuna's withdrawal is not a critique of compassion itself but of compassion detached from the full scope of moral responsibility—compassion that focuses on the immediate emotional cost of action while remaining indifferent to the moral costs of inaction (Ganeri, 2007). The injustice that Arjuna's withdrawal would permit to proceed is not made less real by the sincerity of his reluctance to engage with it.

Krishna's Challenge to Passive Withdrawal

Krishna's teaching to Arjuna is among the most philosophically rich responses to the ethics of duty and force in any tradition. Its central argument is that Arjuna's role—his *svadharma*, the specific duty arising from his nature, training, and position—generates obligations that cannot be dissolved by the discomfort of fulfilling them. The warrior who possesses the capacity to protect righteous order and who abandons that capacity in order to preserve his own emotional comfort has not achieved virtue. He has privileged his personal peace over his moral responsibility (Bhagavad Gita 2:31–33).

This argument does not rest upon a devaluation of human life or an indifference to the costs of conflict. It rests upon a recognition that moral order is fragile—that injustice, left unopposed, does not remain static but expands, corrupts, and destroys the conditions under which peaceful and righteous life is possible. The person capable of interrupting that expansion who declines to do so has made a choice with consequences—consequences that fall not upon themselves but upon those who depended upon their willingness to act.

Why Dharma Requires Action Rather Than Preference

The concept of *nishkama karma*—action without attachment to personal outcome, performed because duty requires it rather than because it produces emotional satisfaction—is among the Gita's most significant ethical contributions. It establishes that the moral legitimacy of an act cannot be determined by whether the person performing it finds it comfortable, desirable, or personally rewarding. Duty is discerned through the honest assessment of obligation, not through the filter of emotional preference.

Applied to defensive force, this principle produces a framework of considerable moral seriousness. The defender who acts from genuine duty—from the obligation to protect those who cannot protect themselves, to preserve the conditions of righteous order against those who would destroy them—is acting from a fundamentally different moral orientation than the person who employs force for personal satisfaction, revenge, or the assertion of power. The Gita insists upon this distinction and evaluates action accordingly.

Force, Tragedy, and Moral Restraint Within Dharma

Why Hindu Ethics Does Not Celebrate Violence

The Bhagavad Gita's permission for righteous force is surrounded by a moral framework that strips it of any celebratory character. Violence arising from ego, from hatred, from the desire for domination or personal gratification, is condemned throughout the text with consistent force.

The *tamasic* qualities—those associated with darkness, ignorance, and moral corruption—include precisely the anger, cruelty, and pride that tend to accompany force deployed without adequate moral governance (Bhagavad Gita 18:25).

The scholar Barbara Stoler Miller, in her analysis of the Gita's ethical framework, argues that the text's permission for force is inseparable from its insistence upon the purification of motive—that righteous action requires the progressive subordination of personal desire, anger, and ego to the demands of duty and the requirements of moral order (Miller, 1986).

Force that serves the self is morally suspect, regardless of how it is rationalized. Force that serves genuine duty, under the discipline of self-mastery and the governance of conscience, occupies a different moral category entirely.

The Difference Between Duty and Desire

The distinction between action arising from duty and action arising from desire is not peripheral to Hindu ethics. It is structural—the axis around which the Gita's entire moral psychology rotates. The righteous defender does not employ force because violence is desired, because injury to the aggressor is sought, or because conflict provides an occasion for the expression of power. They employ it because the obligations generated by their role, their relationships, and their capacity to protect leave no morally adequate alternative.

This means that the internal disposition of the defender—what the tradition calls *bhava*, the emotional and intentional orientation of the actor—is as morally significant as the external act. The person who employs defensive force while maintaining equanimity, without hatred toward the aggressor, without pride in their own capability, and without attachment to the outcome beyond the fulfillment of duty has met the standard the Gita establishes. The person who employs the same force from anger, ego, or the pleasure of domination has not, regardless of whether the external circumstances might otherwise have justified the action (Bhagavad Gita 3:19).

Why Injustice Allowed to Continue Corrupts Moral Order

Hindu philosophy treats moral order—*rita* in the Vedic tradition, *dharma* in its later elaborations—not as a self-sustaining condition but as a fragile achievement requiring active preservation. Injustice unchecked does not simply persist. It expands, corrupts the conditions of righteous life, and draws those who witness it without response into a form of moral complicity that the tradition treats with considerable seriousness.

The philosopher Ram-Prasad Chakravarthi, in his examination of Hindu ethics and political philosophy, observes that the tradition consistently understands inaction in the face of genuine injustice not as neutrality but as a form of participation in the injustice's continuation—a failure of the stewardship obligation that capability generates (Chakravarthi, 2006).

The warrior who abandons the field while injustice advances has not preserved his moral purity. He has redirected the harm toward those less capable of resisting it—and the tradition holds him accountable for that redirection with the same seriousness it would apply to direct harm.

Why Hindu Ethics Rejects Both Violence and Escapist Pacifism

The moral position the Gita occupies is neither the celebration of violence nor the idealization of passive withdrawal. It is the demanding middle ground of disciplined, duty-governed action that accepts the tragic necessity of force when genuine moral obligation requires it, while refusing every form of force that exceeds that necessity or that serves purposes the tradition cannot sanction.

Unrestrained aggression—force arising from ego, hatred, or the desire for domination—violates *dharma* and corrupts the actor who employs it. Passive abandonment of duty—the withdrawal from genuine moral obligation in the name of personal comfort or emotional purity—also violates *dharma* and fails those whose welfare depends upon the fulfillment of that obligation. The righteous path lies between these failures: disciplined action, governed by self-mastery and moral clarity, employed when duty requires it and restrained when it does not (Bhagavad Gita 2:47–48).

Duty, Self-Mastery, and Defensive Responsibility

Why Capability Creates Responsibility Within Dharma

The Hindu ethical framework generates a direct relationship between capability and moral obligation. The person who possesses genuine defensive capacity—physical strength, training, effective tools, and the knowledge to respond effectively to a genuine threat—has not acquired a morally neutral asset that may be employed or withheld according to personal preference. They have acquired a form of responsibility whose weight increases with the vulnerability of those who might benefit from its exercise.

This principle reflects the broader Hindu understanding that the self exists within a web of relationships—to family, community, and the moral order—whose demands cannot be dissolved by the preference for personal comfort or the avoidance of difficult engagement. Strength employed in the disciplined service of protection is not moral corruption within the Hindu framework. It is the expression of *dharma* in the form that circumstance and capability together require (Flood, 1996).

Firearms and the Neutrality of Tools Within Hindu Ethics

Hindu philosophy evaluates action primarily through the lens of intention, discipline, and alignment with *dharma* rather than through categorical judgment of the instruments through which action is expressed. A firearm, within this framework, is morally neutral in itself—neither righteous nor corrupt, independent of the purpose it serves, the intention governing its use, and the discipline with which it is employed.

What the tradition evaluates is not the weapon but the moral agent—the quality of intention, the presence or absence of ego and desire, and the degree to which the action it makes possible aligns with genuine duty rather than personal gratification. The defender who bears a firearm with the equanimity, humility, and moral seriousness that the Gita demands has not compromised their spiritual integrity. They have expressed it in a form that their circumstances and their obligations require. The defender who bears the same instrument from pride, anger, or the desire for domination has failed the tradition's moral standard—not because of the instrument but because of the internal orientation that governs its use.

The Necessity of Internal Discipline and Self-Mastery

The Gita's emphasis on self-mastery—on the conquest of ego, desire, anger, and attachment that the text regards as the precondition for righteous action—is not incidental to its treatment of defensive force. It is central to it. The person who has not developed the internal governance to manage their own emotional states under pressure cannot reliably meet the moral standards that righteous defensive action requires. They cannot distinguish duty from desire, necessity from preference, or the proportionate response from the excessive one, because the ego and emotion that should be subordinated to moral clarity have not been adequately disciplined.

The tradition of *yoga*—understood not merely as physical practice but as the systematic cultivation of self-mastery across all dimensions of the self—is among the Gita's most important prescriptions for anyone who would act rightly under conditions of genuine moral pressure. The warrior who has mastered themselves before the encounter is equipped to maintain the equanimity, discipline, and moral clarity that righteous action demands during it (Easwaran, 2007).

Grief, Reflection, and the Human Cost of Righteous Action

The Bhagavad Gita does not promise that righteous action is painless. Arjuna's grief at the beginning of the text is not resolved by being declared irrelevant. It is transformed—through the dialogue with Krishna—into a grief that can be carried without being paralyzing and acknowledged without becoming an excuse for moral abdication. The tradition recognizes that even action fully aligned with *dharma* may leave emotional and spiritual burdens that the morally serious person must bear with honesty and humility.

Sorrow after conflict is not evidence of moral failure within the Hindu framework. It is evidence of the seriousness with which the actor regards the value of the lives implicated in their choices—including the life of the aggressor whose conduct made defensive action necessary. The person who emerges from genuine defensive necessity without any sense of the weight of what occurred has not achieved spiritual strength. They have achieved a form of moral callousness that the tradition regards as its own kind of corruption. Hindu ethics preserve humanity precisely by insisting that righteous action can still wound the soul—and that the willingness to bear that wound, without either flinching from duty or surrendering to despair, is itself among the marks of genuine moral maturity.

Thoughts to Ponder: Duty Above Comfort

Hindu philosophy teaches that morality is not proven by avoiding burden. It is proven by carrying responsibility without surrendering to hatred, pride, or excess. The Bhagavad Gita's engagement with the ethics of force remains among the most philosophically serious treatments of moral duty under genuine pressure available in any tradition—precisely because it refuses the comfort of simple answers and insists upon the harder work of honest engagement with what dharma actually requires.

Defensive force, within the Hindu framework, is morally legitimate when aligned with genuine duty, governed by self-mastery, and freed from the ego-driven motives that corrupt righteous action into something the tradition cannot sanction. These conditions are demanding. They are designed to be—because the moral stakes of force are real, and the tradition that takes those stakes most seriously is the tradition best equipped to govern them wisely.

The next chapter turns to Buddhism—a tradition whose profound commitment to non-harm places it in the most apparent tension with the ethics of defensive force and whose most serious moral thinkers have nevertheless refused to resolve that tension by pretending it does not exist.

Chapter 12:

Buddhism—Compassion, Harm, and Moral Tragedy

Buddhism is perhaps the tradition most frequently invoked in arguments for absolute non-resistance—and perhaps the tradition most poorly served by that invocation.

The Buddhist commitment to nonviolence is genuine, profound, and among the most carefully developed ethical positions in any major moral tradition. It is also not what its casual appropriators typically present it as being. Buddhism does not deny suffering.

It does not promise that moral life can be navigated without painful choices. It does not treat the mere avoidance of action as equivalent to ethical achievement.

What it offers is something considerably more demanding: a framework for engaging with moral reality—including its most tragic dimensions—with clarity, compassion, and the disciplined awareness that the tradition regards as the foundation of all genuine ethical life.

The question Buddhism must answer honestly is not whether violence is harmful. Its answer to that question is unambiguous.

The question is what compassion actually requires when the available alternatives include not only violence but also the suffering that inaction permits to continue.

Suffering, Compassion, and the Discipline of Nonviolence

Dukkha and the Reality of Human Suffering

Buddhism begins not with an ideal but with a diagnosis. The first of the Four Noble Truths—the foundational framework of Buddhist moral and spiritual teaching—is the acknowledgment of *dukkha*: the pervasive unsatisfactoriness and suffering that characterizes unexamined human existence. This beginning is philosophically significant. A tradition that places the honest acknowledgment of suffering at the center of its moral framework has already committed itself to engaging with reality rather than retreating from it—and that commitment shapes everything that follows in Buddhist ethical reasoning.

Violence, within this framework, is understood as one of the most potent generators of *dukkha*—producing suffering not only for its immediate victims but also for those who employ it, for the communities that witness it, and for the social fabric that sustains human life and the conditions of ethical practice. The Buddhist aversion to violence is not a sentimental preference for pleasantness. It is a carefully reasoned response to an accurate assessment of what violence costs—a cost that extends far beyond the immediate physical harm and ramifies across multiple dimensions of human experience (Gethin, 1998).

Ahimsa and the Commitment to Non-Harm

The principle of *ahimsa*—non-harm—is among the most fundamental commitments in Buddhist ethical life.

It arises not from an abstract rule against violence but from *karuna*—compassion, the direct recognition of suffering in others and the desire to alleviate rather than increase it. The Buddhist practitioner who genuinely perceives the interconnectedness of all suffering—who understands that harming another is not a contained act with localized consequences but a ripple whose effects extend throughout the web of dependent origination—has a natural motivation toward non-harm that runs deeper than rule-following.

This understanding of *ahimsa* has an important implication that is frequently overlooked: it is fundamentally a discipline of mind and intention rather than merely a restriction on external behavior. The person who refrains from physical violence while maintaining active hatred, contempt, or indifference toward others has not achieved *ahimsa* in any meaningful Buddhist sense.

And the person who, in genuinely tragic circumstances, employs minimal necessary force while maintaining compassion toward all parties—including the aggressor—occupies a morally different position than one whose non-action is accompanied by coldness toward those whose suffering they could have prevented (Harvey, 2000).

Why Buddhism Distinguishes Between Outward Action and Inner Motivation

The Buddhist emphasis on *cetana*—intention as the moral core of action—is among the tradition's most significant contributions to ethical thought. The canonical statement attributed to the Buddha—that intention is karma, that it is through intention that one creates moral consequence through body, speech, and mind—establishes that the moral evaluation of any act cannot be determined by the act alone (Anguttara Nikaya 6.63).

The mental state driving the action—whether rooted in the three poisons of hatred, greed, and delusion, or in their opposites of compassion, generosity, and clarity—determines the moral character of what occurs. This principle has profound implications for the ethics of defensive force. It means that the same outward act—the use of force against an aggressor—may occupy radically different moral categories depending upon the mental state from which it arises.

Force arising from hatred, ego, or the desire to dominate generates negative karma regardless of whether the immediate target deserved resistance. Force arising from genuine compassion—from the desire to prevent greater suffering, undertaken reluctantly and without attachment to the act itself—represents an entirely different moral situation that the tradition's evaluative framework must assess differently.

Why Buddhism Does Not Equate Nonviolence With Passive Indifference

The conflation of Buddhist nonviolence with passive indifference to preventable suffering is one of the more serious misreadings of the tradition. Buddhism is not a philosophy of emotional detachment from the world's pain. *Karuna*—compassion—is an active, engaged quality that moves toward suffering rather than away from it, seeking its alleviation through whatever means wisdom and awareness make available.

The scholar Damien Keown, in his careful analysis of Buddhist ethics, argues that the tradition's ethical reasoning is ultimately oriented toward the reduction of suffering rather than toward the preservation of the moral actor's personal purity (Keown, 2001). A Buddhism that prioritized the practitioner's freedom from moral complication over the welfare of those whose suffering could be alleviated or prevented would have fundamentally misunderstood its own foundational commitments. Compassion that refuses engagement with genuine suffering in order to remain untouched by moral complexity is not compassion. It is a form of self-protective indifference wearing compassion's name.

Moral Tragedy, Defensive Action, and the Burden of Consequence

The Bodhisattva Stories and Compassionate Intervention

The Mahayana Buddhist tradition contains a remarkable body of narratives in which Bodhisattvas—beings of profound compassion who have committed themselves to the liberation of all sentient creatures—undertake harmful action to prevent greater suffering.

These stories are not presented as celebrations of violence or as exceptions that effectively nullify the commitment to *ahimsa*. They are presented as illustrations of the moral terrain that genuine compassion must sometimes navigate—terrain in which every available path involves harm, and the question is not how to avoid harm entirely but how to minimize it while bearing the full weight of the consequence.

One of the most significant of these narratives describes a Bodhisattva who kills a murderer to prevent that person from killing hundreds of others—and who accepts the karmic consequence of the killing upon himself in order to spare the would-be murderer the far greater karmic consequence of mass murder (Tatz, 1986).

The moral logic of this narrative is precise and demanding: the harmful action is motivated entirely by compassion toward all parties, including the aggressor. It is undertaken without hatred, without ego, and without any trace of the desire for violence. And the Bodhisattva accepts the moral and karmic cost of the action rather than treating it as a triumph.

This is Buddhist ethics engaging with genuine moral tragedy—not denying it, not escaping it through abstraction, but entering it with full awareness and full compassion.

Why Buddhism Rejects Moral Simplicity

The existence of such narratives in the Buddhist canon is itself philosophically significant. A tradition committed to the absolute prohibition of harmful action under any circumstances would have no use for these stories.

Their presence reflects the tradition's honest acknowledgment that moral reality is not always structured to permit clean solutions—that some situations present genuine dilemmas in which every available choice involves harm, and in which the ethical question is not whether harm can be avoided but how it can be minimized and how its unavoidable remainder can be borne with the appropriate moral seriousness.

The philosopher Charles Goodman, in his analysis of Buddhist ethics and consequential reasoning, argues that the Mahayana tradition in particular has consistently recognized that the reduction of overall suffering—the alleviation of *dukkha* across the full scope of those affected by a moral situation—must sometimes take precedence over the preservation of the individual practitioner's personal non-involvement in harm (Goodman, 2009).

Avoiding action does not always reduce suffering.

Sometimes it permits suffering to expand in ways that genuine compassion cannot accept without moral compromise.

The Importance of Mental State During Defensive Force

The Buddhist framework's emphasis on mental state as the determinant of moral character produces a nuanced and demanding standard for defensive action. Force arising from hatred—even force directed against a genuine aggressor—deepens suffering in ways that extend beyond the immediate physical harm. It reinforces the mental habits of aggression, damages the practitioner's capacity for compassion, and generates karmic consequences that the tradition regards with seriousness.

Force undertaken reluctantly, from genuine concern for the welfare of all parties—including the aggressor—and without attachment to the act itself or its outcome, occupies a fundamentally different moral space. The mental discipline required to maintain this orientation under conditions of genuine threat and genuine fear is among the most demanding things Buddhist practice can ask of a practitioner. It requires not merely the technical capacity for effective response, but the depth of compassionate awareness and ego dissolution that sustained practice cultivates—the ability to act from clarity rather than from the reactive emotional states that threatening situations naturally generate (Thich Nhat Hanh, 1987).

Why Tragedy Does Not Eliminate Moral Responsibility

Buddhism does not promise that righteous action produces morally painless outcomes. The acceptance of *dukkha* as a fundamental feature of existence includes the acceptance that moral life will sometimes require choices whose consequences are genuinely painful—to others, to the practitioner, to the web of relationships within which all human action occurs. The appropriate response to this reality is not despair, not the search for a purity that the world's actual moral complexity does not permit, and not the abdication of responsibility in favor of the appearance of non-involvement.

The appropriate response, within the Buddhist framework, is *sati*—mindfulness: the clear, compassionate awareness of what is occurring, what one's choices will produce, and what the full range of those affected by one's action and inaction will experience as a consequence. The practitioner who employs defensive force with this quality of awareness—who sees clearly what is happening, acts from compassion rather than from hatred, and carries the moral weight of the outcome with humility and honest acknowledgment—has met the tradition's most demanding standard. Not because the outcome was good, but because the consciousness that generated it was as free as possible from the poisons that transform genuine moral tragedy into moral failure.

Mindfulness, Restraint, and Defensive Responsibility

Why Buddhism Rejects the Idea That Helplessness Equals Virtue

The Buddhist tradition does not identify moral achievement with incapacity. The Bodhisattva ideal—the being of extraordinary compassion and wisdom toward whom Mahayana practice orients—is not a figure of weakness or helplessness.

It is a figure of immense capability placed entirely in the service of compassion for all sentient beings. What distinguishes the Bodhisattva morally is not the absence of power but the complete subordination of that power to compassionate purpose.

This distinction matters practically. A person genuinely incapable of an effective response to violence is not demonstrating *ahimsa.* They are simply operating at the limits of their capability. The moral achievement that *ahimsa* represents requires the actual capacity to cause harm—and the disciplined, compassionate choice to minimize that harm to what genuine necessity requires.

Moral seriousness, within the Buddhist framework, emerges precisely where genuine capability exists and is governed by the awareness, compassion, and restraint that the tradition cultivates (Harvey, 2000).

Firearms as Morally Neutral Instruments

Buddhist moral reasoning evaluates the consciousness, employing a tool rather than the tool itself. A firearm, within this framework, is morally inert—neither righteous nor corrupt, independent of the mental state and intention of the person using it. The tradition's emphasis on *cetana* places moral responsibility entirely within the practitioner rather than distributing it across the objects they employ.

This means that the same instrument can occupy radically different moral positions depending upon the mind that directs it.

Used from hatred, ego, or the pleasure of domination, it generates the karma of harmful action regardless of whether the immediate target was a genuine aggressor.

Used reluctantly, from genuine compassion toward all affected parties, with clear awareness of necessity and proportionality, and without attachment to the act or its outcome, it represents a different moral situation entirely.

The tradition's evaluative framework is not indifferent to this difference. It is built around it.

The Ethical Necessity of Humility and Reflection

The Buddhist tradition's insistence on mindfulness—the continuous, clear awareness of one's mental states, intentions, and the consequences they generate—extends beyond the moment of action into the period that follows it. Defensive force, even when genuinely necessary and compassionately motivated, should produce in the practitioner not satisfaction or pride but the sober, humble acknowledgment of what has occurred and what it has cost.

Remorse, within the Buddhist framework, is not the same as guilt. Guilt is self-focused—a form of ego-attachment to the image of oneself as a person who does not cause harm.

Remorse is other-focused—a compassionate acknowledgment of the suffering that has occurred, including the suffering of the person against whom force was necessary. The capacity to carry this acknowledgment with honesty and without either self-condemnation or self-justification is among the marks of the mindfulness that genuine Buddhist practice cultivates.

It guards against the moral numbness that repeated exposure to violence can produce—the progressive dulling of the compassionate awareness that the tradition regards as the practitioner's most important moral resource.

Why Buddhism Resists Both Denial and Indulgence

The Buddhist path—the *majjhima patipada*, the middle way—is defined by its refusal of extremes. Applied to the ethics of defensive force, this principle generates a position that resists with equal firmness both the denial of moral complexity and the indulgence of violence. Buddhism neither pretends that defensive force is morally simple nor celebrates it as an acceptable expression of strength. It insists upon the full moral weight of what force costs—and then asks whether, in specific circumstances of genuine necessity and genuine compassion, that cost can be accepted without the hatred, ego, and attachment that would transform a tragic moral necessity into a moral failure.

The answer the tradition offers is neither simple permission nor simple prohibition. It is the demand for the kind of consciousness—clear, compassionate, humble, mindful of consequence—that alone can navigate genuine moral tragedy without adding to the suffering it was unable to prevent.

Thoughts to Ponder: Compassion Under Burden

Buddhism contributes to the broader moral framework of this book something that no other tradition provides in quite the same way: an insistence that the ethical quality of defensive force is located primarily in the consciousness from which it arises rather than in the act itself. This insistence does not dissolve the moral seriousness of force. It deepens it by requiring not merely correct behavior under pressure but the kind of inner formation that makes correct behavior possible when hatred, fear, and ego are all pulling in other directions. Buddhist ethics does not seek moral purity through avoidance of complexity. It seeks wisdom, awareness, and the reduction of suffering within an imperfect world that does not always offer morally comfortable choices. The practitioner who can act from genuine compassion in genuinely tragic circumstances—without hatred, without pride, and without attachment to the outcome—and who carries the weight of that action with the humility and mindfulness the tradition demands has achieved something that the tradition regards as among the most difficult and most significant moral accomplishments available to human beings.

The next chapter turns to Sikhism—a tradition that has perhaps most explicitly and deliberately integrated the demand for spiritual depth with the obligation of protective readiness, producing in the ideal of the saint-soldier one of the most philosophically serious models of disciplined, defensive responsibility in the history of moral thought.

Chapter 13:

Sikhism—The Saint-Soldier Ideal

Sikhism presents one of the most philosophically integrated responses to the tension between spiritual devotion and defensive responsibility available in any major religious tradition.

Where other traditions tend to hold these commitments in productive tension—acknowledging that force and spirituality pull against each other and seeking principled ways to navigate the friction—Sikhism insists that the tension is itself a misunderstanding.

Genuine spiritual development, within the Sikh framework, produces not the retreat from worldly responsibility but its fullest acceptance.

The saint and the soldier are not competing ideals requiring uneasy compromise. They are two dimensions of a single moral achievement, each incomplete without the other.

This integration did not emerge from theoretical reflection conducted at a safe distance from the realities it addresses.

It emerged from direct historical confrontation with persecution, oppression, and the lived experience of communities for whom the question of defensive responsibility was not academic but existential.

Sikh moral reasoning bears the marks of that confrontation—and is more honest, more practically serious, and more philosophically coherent for having been shaped by it.

The Saint-Soldier and the Moral Duty to Defend

The Meaning of the Saint-Soldier Ideal

The concept of the *Sant-Sipahi*—the saint-soldier—is among the most distinctive and morally significant contributions Sikhism makes to the broader conversation about ethics, force, and human responsibility.

It names a specific form of moral integration: the person who has developed, through sustained spiritual practice, the humility, compassion, and devotion that genuine holiness requires—and who has simultaneously accepted the obligation to translate those interior qualities into courageous, disciplined action in the defense of justice and the protection of the vulnerable.

What makes this ideal philosophically serious is what it refuses. It refuses the separation of spiritual achievement from practical responsibility—the comfortable position that genuine holiness is demonstrated by withdrawal from the world's difficult demands rather than by engagement with them.

And it refuses the opposite error with equal firmness: the glorification of courage and strength detached from the spiritual discipline that alone can prevent them from becoming instruments of ego, pride, or domination. The saint without courage, in the Sikh understanding, is spiritually incomplete—possessing inner cultivation without the willingness to act upon it when action is morally required. The soldier without sanctity is morally dangerous—possessing capability without the conscience and restraint that give capability its ethical character (Singh, 2005).

Sikhism's Historical Context of Oppression and Resistance

Sikh ethical thought did not develop in conditions of security and comfort. The tradition emerged in the Punjab of the sixteenth and seventeenth centuries under conditions of political instability and religious persecution that gave its moral reasoning an urgency and a concreteness that purely theoretical ethics rarely achieves. The martyrdom of Guru Arjan Dev in 1606 and Guru Tegh Bahadur in 1675—both executed by Mughal authorities—were not merely historical events. They were formative moral experiences that shaped the tradition's understanding of what justice requires and what the cost of standing between the vulnerable and oppression actually looks like.

The historian Nikky-Guninder Kaur Singh, in her examination of Sikh theology and practice, argues that this historical context is inseparable from the tradition's moral conclusions—that Sikhism's ethical framework was not imposed upon its historical experience but grew directly from it, producing a moral realism that refused the luxury of abstraction precisely because the communities that shaped it could not afford it (Kaur Singh, 2004). Sikh moral reasoning addresses the world as it exists—containing genuine injustice, genuine persecution, and the genuine suffering of people who need protection—rather than the world as an idealized moral framework might prefer it to be.

Why Sikh Ethics Rejects Passive Submission to Injustice

The Sikh tradition is explicit in its rejection of passive submission to oppression. This rejection is not a concession to pragmatic necessity that sits uneasily alongside the tradition's deeper spiritual commitments. It is the expression of those commitments—a direct consequence of what Sikhism understands genuine devotion to require.

The concept of *seva*—selfless service—is among the most fundamental practices in Sikh religious life. It expresses the recognition that genuine spiritual development cannot be contained within private cultivation but must overflow into active concern for the welfare of others. Applied to the reality of injustice and oppression, *seva* generates precisely the protective obligation that the saint-soldier ideal embodies.

Allowing injustice to proceed unchallenged when the capacity to resist it exists is not spiritual detachment within the Sikh framework. It is the failure of the very compassion and service orientation that spiritual practice is designed to cultivate (Cole & Sambhi, 1995).

Spiritual Discipline as Preparation for Moral Responsibility

The relationship between spiritual practice and defensive readiness in Sikhism is not incidental. It is structural. The discipline of *simran*—meditative remembrance of the divine—cultivates the inner qualities that righteous action under pressure requires: the equanimity that prevents fear from corrupting judgment, the humility that prevents success from generating pride, the compassion that prevents necessary force from becoming hatred, and the clarity that distinguishes genuine duty from ego-driven rationalization.

This means that within the Sikh framework, spiritual practice is not an alternative to practical preparation for moral responsibility. It is the foundation upon which genuine moral responsibility is built. The person who has not cultivated these interior qualities cannot be relied upon to exercise defensive capability with the discipline and restraint that righteous action requires—because under the pressure of genuine conflict, the untrained inner life defaults to its most reactive and least morally reliable states. Devotion and readiness are not competing demands. They are sequential necessities, the first preparing the character for what the second requires.

The Khalsa, Restraint, and Righteous Defense

Guru Gobind Singh and the Formation of the Khalsa

The founding of the Khalsa by Guru Gobind Singh in 1699 represents the most deliberate institutionalization of the saint-soldier ideal in Sikh history—and one of the most philosophically interesting attempts in any tradition to formalize the integration of spiritual commitment and defensive responsibility into a coherent collective identity. The Khalsa was not established as a military organization in the ordinary sense. It was established as a moral community—a disciplined fellowship of individuals who had committed themselves simultaneously to the pursuit of spiritual excellence and to the acceptance of the obligation to defend justice and protect the vulnerable (McLeod, 1989).

The requirements of Khalsa membership—the five *kakars*, the code of conduct, and the commitment to both prayer and preparedness—were not arbitrary institutional requirements. They were designed to produce and sustain the specific type of person that the saint-soldier ideal describes: Someone whose capability for defensive action is inseparable from the spiritual discipline that governs it and whose willingness to employ that capability is inseparable from the humility and restraint that prevent it from becoming something the tradition cannot sanction.

Why Sikhism Treats Force as a Last Resort

The Sikh tradition's willingness to engage with the reality of defensive force is not a willingness to treat force as anything other than a last resort preceded by the exhaustion of every peaceful alternative. Guru Gobind Singh's own formulation—that the sword should be drawn only when all other means have failed—establishes a clear moral priority: peaceful resolution is always the preferred path, and force becomes morally permissible only when that path has been genuinely closed (Guru Gobind Singh, *Zafarnama*, cited in Mandair, 2013).

This insistence on last resort is not a bureaucratic qualification attached reluctantly to an otherwise enthusiastic engagement with conflict. It reflects the tradition's foundational understanding that violence is always costly—to those who suffer it, to those who employ it, and to the fabric of human community within which both exist. The Sikh acceptance of defensive force as sometimes morally necessary is accompanied by a consistent insistence that this necessity is tragic rather than triumphant—that the need for force represents a moral failure at the social and political level, even when the individual who employs it is acting with full moral legitimacy.

Why Restraint Defines Moral Legitimacy

The Sikh ethical framework's commitment to restraint in the exercise of defensive force is as emphatic as its commitment to readiness. The tradition condemns cruelty, revenge, the humiliation of opponents, and the continuation of force beyond what genuine necessity requires with a consistency that reflects its foundational understanding of what defensive action is for. Force that serves justice—that interrupts injustice and protects the vulnerable—retains its moral legitimacy. Force that serves ego, satisfies grievance, or expresses domination has exceeded the boundaries within which the tradition's permission operates.

The scholar Gurinder Singh Mann, in his analysis of Sikh ethics and practice, argues that the tradition's understanding of righteous force is inseparable from its understanding of righteous character—that the same spiritual development that prepares a person for defensive action also governs how that action is conducted and when it must cease (Mann, 2004). The defender who cannot maintain this governance under the pressure of actual conflict has not achieved the integration of saint and soldier that the tradition holds as its moral ideal. They have achieved one at the expense of the other—and the resulting imbalance is precisely what the Sikh framework identifies as the source of moral corruption in the exercise of force.

The Moral Equality of Those Worth Defending

One of the most historically significant dimensions of the Sikh saint-soldier ideal is its explicitly universal scope. The protection that the tradition's moral framework generates is not restricted to the Sikh community.

Guru Tegh Bahadur's martyrdom—his execution following his defense of the religious freedom of Kashmiri Hindus facing forced conversion—is among the most striking illustrations in any religious tradition of the principle that protective obligation is not limited by communal loyalty but extends to anyone facing injustice regardless of their relationship to the defender. This universality is not incidental to the Sikh ethical framework. It follows directly from the tradition's theological conviction that the divine light—*Waheguru*—is present in every human being, making every person deserving of the dignity and protection that genuine moral seriousness requires. The saint-soldier does not protect only their own. They protect because injustice itself violates the moral order that the divine presence in every person demands be honored—and that violation is equally wrong regardless of whose community it falls upon.

Strength, Stewardship, and Defensive Capability

Why Sikhism Rejects the Idea That Virtue Equals Weakness

The Sikh moral framework is among the most explicit of any major religious tradition in its rejection of the identification of spiritual virtue with cultivated incapacity. The saint-soldier ideal is, at its core, a sustained argument against this identification—an insistence that genuine holiness is not demonstrated by the inability to act effectively in the world but by the disciplined, humble, compassionate exercise of genuine capability in service of justice and protection.

Strength, within this framework, becomes virtuous not by being minimized or disguised but by being subordinated to the conscience and the service orientation that spiritual development cultivates. The Khalsa member who possesses genuine defensive capability and governs it with humility, restraint, and compassion has achieved something morally significant precisely because the alternative—the misuse of that capability for ego, domination, or revenge—was genuinely available and genuinely refused. Virtue demonstrated under conditions where no other option existed is not virtue in the morally weighty sense. It is merely the description of a limitation.

Firearms and the Sikh Understanding of Moral Agency

The Sikh tradition's approach to the tools of defensive capability reflects its broader framework for evaluating action through the lens of purpose, intention, and moral governance rather than through categorical judgment of specific instruments.

The tradition's five articles of faith include the *kirpan*—a blade—whose presence is not incidental but symbolic; it represents the obligation to defend justice and protect the vulnerable that Khalsa membership entails. This symbolism reflects a tradition that has never treated defensive capability as inherently corrupting.

A firearm, within the Sikh ethical framework, is evaluated by the same standards applied to every other instrument of defensive capability: does its possession and use serve the protection of innocent life? Is it governed by the necessity, proportionality, and restraint that righteous action requires? Is it derived from the service orientation of the saint-soldier or from the ego-driven motivations that the tradition condemns?

These questions do not produce categorical answers about specific technologies. They produce a moral framework within which any instrument of defensive capability can be assessed according to the principles that Sikh ethics consistently applies—principles oriented toward the protection of the vulnerable, the restraint of the capable, and the accountability of the powerful before the divine presence they are called to honor (Nesbitt, 2005).

Preparedness as Responsibility Rather Than Paranoia

Sikh ethics frames defensive preparedness not as an expression of fear or aggression but as a dimension of the service obligation that genuine moral seriousness generates. The Khalsa member who maintains readiness does so not because they are seeking conflict or because they distrust their neighbors, but because they have accepted an obligation toward the protection of the vulnerable that readiness is a precondition for fulfilling. Preparedness, understood in this way, is an act of humility rather than pride—the acknowledgment that the world contains genuine injustice and that the person capable of responding to it has a responsibility to ensure that their response, when it becomes necessary, will be adequate.

This framing has direct implications for how the tradition evaluates the investment in training, the maintenance of capability, and the acceptance of the burden that genuine defensive readiness involves. These are not expressions of martial enthusiasm within the Sikh framework. They are expressions of the service ethic—of the willingness to bear the cost and the responsibility of capability in order to fulfill the obligation to protect that the saint-soldier ideal generates.

Sacrifice, Humility, and the Cost of Defense

The Sikh tradition honors sacrifice without romanticizing violence—maintaining a clear and consistent distinction between the courage and burden-bearing that genuine protective responsibility requires and the glorification of conflict that the tradition consistently refuses. The martyrs of Sikh history are honored not because they were warriors who prevailed in battle but because they were willing to bear the ultimate cost of standing between injustice and those who could not protect themselves. Their example is held up not as inspiration for aggression but as the standard of what genuine service to justice, conducted without hatred and without self-glorification, actually looks like in practice.

Humility after conflict—the recognition that what has occurred, however necessary, carries moral and spiritual weight that honest acknowledgment requires—is as important within the Sikh ethical framework as the courage that engagement required. The saint-soldier who emerges from defensive necessity with pride rather than sober awareness of what the conflict cost has lost something essential. The tradition's insistence on this humility is not weakness. It is the spiritual discipline that prevents the justified use of force from becoming the beginning of something the tradition cannot sanction.

Thoughts to Ponder: Courage Governed by Conscience

Sikhism offers to the moral conversation of this book something irreplaceable: the demonstration that spiritual depth and defensive readiness are not merely compatible but mutually necessary—that the cultivation of one without the other produces either the ineffective holiness of the saint who cannot protect or the dangerous capability of the soldier without conscience. The saint-soldier ideal insists upon both, at the full demanding standard that both require.

Peace, within the Sikh framework, is not preserved through passive hope. It is preserved through disciplined individuals willing to stand between injustice and the vulnerable—governed by conscience, restrained by the spiritual formation that prevents capability from becoming corruption, and humble enough to bear the burden of what protection costs without allowing that burden to generate either pride or bitterness. That willingness, held together with the devotion and compassion that give it its moral character, is the Sikh tradition's enduring answer to the question of what genuine moral seriousness about the protection of innocent life actually requires.

PART IV

Firearms as Moral Instruments

(Chapters 14-17)

The possession of arms is the distinction between a freeman and a slave.
— James Burgh

Chapter 14:

Why Firearms Changed the Moral Equation

The moral questions surrounding self-defense did not originate with firearms. They originated with human vulnerability—with the fact, as old as the species itself, that human beings can be unjustly harmed by other human beings and must decide what to do about it. What firearms changed was not the existence of that problem but the practical distribution of the capacity to address it. They altered who could meaningfully participate in their own defense, who could protect those in their care, and who could stand between the vulnerable and those willing to use force against them. That redistribution of agency is not a trivial technological fact. It is a moral development whose implications have been imperfectly understood precisely because the conversation surrounding it has focused on the instrument rather than on what the instrument actually changed.

Before Firearms: Defense as the Privilege of Strength

The Historical Relationship Between Power and Physical Strength

For most of human history, defensive capability was inseparable from physical capability. The person who could defend themselves and those they were responsible for was, in practical terms, the person who was larger, stronger, younger, more numerous, or better positioned to absorb and inflict physical harm in close combat. This was not merely a tactical fact.

It was a moral reality with consequences that the formal recognition of equal human worth could do relatively little to address.

Feudal social structures were organized, at least partly, around the practical reality that personal protection required either the physical capacity to fight or access to someone else who possessed it.

The knight, the retainer, the armed nobleman—these were responses to a practical situation in which the ability to resist violence was unevenly distributed, and in which those who lacked defensive capability were genuinely dependent upon those who possessed it (Keeley, 1996).

Moral equality may have been affirmed in theological and philosophical frameworks. Practical defensibility was another matter entirely.

Why Defensive Capacity Matters Morally

The gap between the formal recognition of a right and the practical capacity to exercise it is not a philosophical technicality. It is a moral problem of considerable seriousness.

A person who possesses, in principle, the right to preserve their life but who lacks any meaningful capacity to do so when genuinely threatened has a right that is, in practice, nearly empty.

The moral traditions examined throughout this book—the Jewish emphasis on *pikuach nefesh*, the natural law argument for pre-political rights, and the Stoic insistence on duty as a function of genuine capability—all presuppose that the rights they affirm can be meaningfully exercised by those who hold them.

The elderly person confronted by a stronger aggressor, the single person facing multiple attackers, the individual beyond the reach of institutional assistance—these are not marginal exceptions.

They are precisely the cases in which the gap between formal right and practical capacity becomes most visible, most consequential, and most morally urgent (Lott, 2000).

The question of whether a meaningful means of defense is available to people facing genuine threats is not separable from the moral framework affirming their right to defend themselves. It is internal to that framework.

Firearms and the Equalization of Defensive Power

The introduction of firearms disrupted the relationship between physical dominance and defensive capability. Firearms reduced the decisive importance of size, strength, age, and proximity—making an effective defensive response accessible to people who would, under earlier technological conditions, have had little practical ability to resist a physically superior aggressor.

This equalization is not incidental to the moral significance of firearms. It is central to it. The philosopher John Lott identifies the equalizing function of firearms as among their most morally significant characteristics—their capacity to translate the formal moral equality of human beings into something closer to a practical equality of defensive capacity that earlier technologies could not achieve (Lott, 2000). This does not resolve every moral question surrounding firearms.

It establishes why those questions cannot be adequately addressed without acknowledging what firearms actually changed in the relationship between moral right and practical capacity.

Why This Redistribution Created Moral Discomfort

The redistribution of defensive capability that firearms produced was not universally welcomed, and the discomfort it generated was not always, or even primarily, moral in origin.

When defensive capability is concentrated in the physically dominant or institutionally protected, its distribution is predictable.

The broader distribution that firearms made possible introduced a form of unpredictability that those accustomed to concentrated capability found genuinely unsettling.

This discomfort was frequently expressed in moral language—in arguments about the dangers of placing destructive power in the hands of ordinary people. But discomfort with the redistribution of power and moral objection to it are not the same thing.

Expanded defensive agency did create expanded moral responsibility, and that expansion was genuinely demanding.

Whether it was genuinely objectionable is a different question requiring a different analysis.

Firearms and the Intensification of Moral Responsibility

Why Firearms Changed Responsibility More Than Violence Itself

The disruption that firearms introduced into human moral experience was not primarily a disruption of the level of violence in human communities. Violence at scale predates firearms by the full extent of recorded history. What firearms changed was the relationship between individual agency and the capacity to prevent harm, making effective defensive responses accessible to people who had previously lacked it and making the question of whether to prepare for a genuine threat a matter of individual moral decision rather than physical circumstance.

This shift placed a new kind of moral demand upon individuals. The person who could not effectively defend themselves under pre-firearms conditions was not making a moral decision in remaining defenseless—they were accepting a practical reality. The person who possesses access to a meaningful means of defense and chooses not to prepare for its responsible use is making a different kind of choice—one with potential consequences for others that the moral frameworks examined throughout this book consistently treat as significant.

The Relationship Between Capability and Obligation

The connection between capability and moral obligation is among the most consistent patterns in the history of ethical thought. The traditions examined in preceding chapters—from the Jewish insistence that *pikuach nefesh* generates duty rather than mere permission, to the Stoic argument that restraint requires genuine capacity, to the Hindu framework in which *svadharma* increases with capability—all reflect the same moral logic: that the possession of means to prevent injustice places the one who possesses those means in a different moral relationship to that injustice than the one who lacks them.

Firearms intensify this relationship by making defensive capability more widely accessible. Where fewer people possessed meaningful defensive capacity, the number of people for whom the capability-obligation connection was practically relevant was correspondingly limited. Where that capacity is more broadly distributed, the moral questions it generates are correspondingly more broadly applicable. This intensification is not a reason to regard firearms with hostility. It is a reason to regard the responsibility their possession generates with the seriousness it deserves (Kleck, 1997).

Why Firearms Force Personal Moral Clarity

One of the more significant effects of firearms as defensive tools is the directness with which they eliminate moral distance between the individual and the question of their own defensive responsibility.

Earlier defensive arrangements—collective protection, physical hierarchy, and institutional reliance—allowed many people to navigate their lives without directly confronting the moral questions surrounding genuine threat and personal response.

Firearms, by making effective individual defensive capacity practically available, transform the choice of whether to accept that capacity and the responsibility it carries into a genuinely personal moral decision.

The psychologist Dave Grossman argues that the willingness to engage honestly with these questions—rather than avoiding them through the comfortable assumption that institutional protection will always be adequate—is itself a dimension of the moral seriousness that genuine responsibility requires (Grossman, 1995). Firearms do not create that seriousness.

They make it unavoidable.

Why Discomfort Is Often Mistaken for Ethical Objection

The discomfort that many people experience in relation to firearms and the direct confrontation with personal defensive responsibility it produces is a genuine psychological phenomenon deserving honest acknowledgment.

What it is not, in itself, is a moral argument. Emotional discomfort and ethical objection are not the same thing, and the failure to distinguish them has produced significant confusion in public discussions of defensive capability.

The discomfort that accompanies genuine moral responsibility—the recognition that capability carries consequence, that preparedness choices have potential implications for others, that defensive force involves moral weight that does not dissolve even when the cause is just—is not evidence that something has gone wrong. It is evidence that the moral seriousness of the situation has been recognized.

That recognition is not a reason to avoid defensive capability. It is a reason to approach it with the discipline, restraint, and character formation that genuine responsibility requires.

Deterrence, Preparedness, and the Ethics of Capability

The Moral Importance of Deterrence

The most morally significant outcomes of defensive capability are frequently invisible. The assault that did not occur because the potential victim's defensive capacity was known; the intrusion abandoned because the risk exceeded the anticipated benefit; the escalation that never happened because the capacity to resist it existed—these prevented harms are genuine moral goods whose significance is not diminished by the absence of a visible event.

This invisibility creates a systematic bias in how defensive capability is evaluated. Harms that firearms prevent leave no statistical trace. Harms that firearms are involved in producing are documented and publicized. Any honest moral accounting must grapple with the full picture—including prevented harms—rather than focusing exclusively on the visible record that the distribution of attention makes most accessible (Kleck, 1997). Deterrence is not a secondary benefit of defensive capability. It is one of its primary moral functions, and a moral framework that cannot acknowledge it has not engaged honestly with the full range of consequences that capability produces.

Firearms and the Exposure of Institutional Limits

Among the more important contributions that honest reflection on firearms makes to the broader ethics of defense is its capacity to reveal the practical limits of institutional protection. Response times vary enormously. Geographic isolation places real limits on how quickly institutional assistance can arrive. System failures during disasters and civil disruptions are historically documented with sufficient frequency to prevent the assumption of universal institutional reliability from serving as an adequate moral foundation for defensive planning.

Firearms do not create these vulnerabilities. They reveal them by making visible the gap between the aspiration of universal institutional protection and the practical reality of its limits. The moral implications of this revelation require the acknowledgment that individual defensive capability is not a redundancy where institutions provide adequate protection but a genuine necessity in a world where that protection is unavoidably incomplete and unevenly distributed (Kopel, 1992).

Why Collective Safety and Individual Preparedness Are Not Opposites

The framing of individual defensive preparedness and collective institutional protection as competing rather than complementary goods is among the more persistent and least defensible assumptions in popular discussions of firearms. Institutional protection and individual capability address different dimensions of the same underlying problem—and the effectiveness of each is not diminished by the existence of the other.

Institutional structures address the broad systemic conditions affecting overall levels of violence in a community. Individual defensive preparedness addresses the immediate reality of specific situations in which institutional protection is unavailable, delayed, or inadequate.

These are complementary functions, not competing ones. The community that invests in both is better protected than the community that invests in either alone, and the moral framework insisting upon treating them as alternatives has manufactured a conflict that the actual structure of the problem does not require.

Firearms as Revelations of Character Rather Than Sources of Corruption

The most important moral observation about firearms is one that recurs throughout the traditions examined in this book in various formulations: tools do not manufacture moral character. They reveal it.

The reckless person who handles a firearm recklessly was reckless before they encountered it. The disciplined person who handles it with the gravity its consequences demand was disciplined before accepting the responsibility its possession entails.

What firearms do—with unusual efficiency and consequence—is reduce the margin for the casual thoughtlessness that other domains of life sometimes absorb without catastrophic results.

They insist upon the concreteness of moral choice and the permanence of its consequences in ways that tools with less severe effects do not. They make visible, with uncomfortable speed, whether the person bearing them possesses the judgment, restraint, and moral formation that responsible use requires.

The moral challenge this creates is not an argument against their defensive use. It is an argument for taking seriously, in advance, the character formation that their defensive use demands.

Thoughts to Ponder: Modern Capability and Ancient Responsibility

Firearms did not change the foundational moral questions surrounding self-defense. They changed who could meaningfully participate in answering them. By redistributing defensive capability more broadly than any previous technology had achieved, they transformed the ethics of defense from a question primarily relevant to those with physical dominance or institutional access into one that touches the lives of ordinary people across every condition of vulnerability. That transformation intensified moral responsibility without altering its fundamental structure—the same questions of necessity, proportionality, restraint, and character that governed the ethics of defensive force before firearms remain the questions that govern it after them.

The moral challenge that firearms present is not the existence of force. Force was present before them and would persist without them. The challenge is whether individuals who bear the expanded defensive capability they provide possess the discipline, restraint, and moral accountability required to govern that capability responsibly—and whether the broader culture takes seriously enough the character formation that genuine responsibility of this kind demands.

Chapter 15:

Firearms and Moral Distance

One of the more persistent intuitions in popular moral reasoning about firearms is the belief that distance makes defensive force less legitimate—that there is something ethically cleaner about close-range resistance, something more authentic about a defender who must physically grapple with a threat rather than respond to it from a distance. This intuition feels morally serious. It connects to deep human associations between proximity and genuine engagement, between physical struggle and honest confrontation. It is also, upon careful examination, more emotional than ethical—a confusion of psychological discomfort with moral principle that does not survive scrutiny.

The question this chapter asks is precise: Does physical distance reduce moral accountability, or does it merely alter the mechanics through which defense is exercised? The answer that serious ethical analysis produces is equally precise. Distance changes tactics. It does not change the moral structure within which those tactics must be evaluated.

Distance Has Always Been Part of Defense

The Historical Presence of Distance in Defensive Practices

The association of firearms with the introduction of distance into defensive ethics reflects a historical amnesia about how defense has actually been practiced across human civilization.

Distance has been a feature of protective action since the earliest recoverable evidence of organized human communities confronting external threats. The archer defending a settlement from a fortified wall, the sentinel observing approaching danger from an elevated position, the shepherd driving off predators from a distance to protect livestock—these are not exotic exceptions to a historical norm of intimate defensive engagement. They are among the most consistent patterns in the history of human protective action.

Ancient military history is substantially a history of distance as defensive strategy. The longbow gave English archers at Agincourt the capacity to defend against cavalry charges from ranges that close combat could not have managed. Roman siege warfare involved the systematic use of projectile weapons precisely to neutralize threats before they could inflict the casualties that close engagement would require.

The Mongol cavalry's devastating effectiveness rested substantially upon archery conducted at distances that prevented effective counterattack (Keeley, 1996). In none of these cases did the moral traditions of the societies employing these methods treat the presence of distance as a disqualifying feature of their defensive legitimacy.

Why Moral Traditions Never Required Physical Proximity

The ethical systems that have governed the use of defensive force across human history—the just war tradition, natural law reasoning, and the religious frameworks examined in preceding chapters—have consistently evaluated force according to criteria of intention, necessity, justice, and restraint. None of them have included physical proximity as a determinant of moral legitimacy.

The archer defending innocent life from a fortified position was not considered less morally serious than the foot soldier engaging in hand-to-hand combat.

The criterion was never how close the defender stood to the threat. It was whether the force employed served the protective purpose that justified its use.

This is not an oversight in the moral tradition. It reflects a correct understanding of where moral responsibility actually resides. Duty to protect does not diminish with geographic distance from the person being protected. The obligation of a parent to their child does not weaken because physical separation prevents intimate engagement with the threat.

The sentinel's responsibility to warn and defend the community they are positioned to protect is not less serious because their action occurs from a distance (Walzer, 1977). Moral responsibility follows intention and action, not measured physical proximity.

The Difference Between Emotional Closeness and Moral Accountability

The confusion between emotional experience and ethical validity is understandable but consequential. Close-range confrontation is viscerally immediate in ways that distance is not.

The emotional intensity of physical struggle—the direct, unmediated experience of danger and response—carries a psychological weight that influences how we perceive the moral seriousness of an act. But psychological intensity and ethical legitimacy are not the same thing, and substituting the first for the second produces moral reasoning governed by emotional symbolism rather than by the principles that serious ethical thought requires. The moralist who insists that close-range defense is inherently more legitimate than ranged defense has allowed an aesthetic preference for physical authenticity to masquerade as a moral argument. The person defending their life from a distance is not less morally engaged than the person defending it at close range.

They are differently situated—and the moral evaluation of their action depends upon the same considerations that apply in every other case: whether the force was genuine, necessary, proportionate, and directed at protection rather than at any of the morally disqualifying alternatives.

Why Prevention Is Morally Preferable to Escalation

Distance frequently allows threats to be addressed at an earlier stage of their development—before the physical escalation that intimate confrontation requires has occurred, and before the injuries that such escalation produces have been inflicted.

A threat stopped at distance before it reaches the point of physical domination is not a threat stopped in a morally inferior way. It is, in most cases, a threat stopped with less harm to all parties than would have resulted from allowing it to develop to the point where close-range resistance was the only remaining option.

The moral traditions examined throughout this book consistently emphasize the priority of preserving innocent life—and if distance enables threats to be neutralized with less overall harm, that reduction in harm is itself a moral consideration of genuine weight.

Prevention is not a morally inferior substitute for heroic close-range struggle.

Within the framework of any tradition that takes seriously the preservation of innocent life, prevention is preferable—and the capacity to achieve it at a distance is a feature rather than a defect of the defensive tool that enables it.

Distance Does Not Eliminate Moral Responsibility

Why Accountability Is Not Measured in Feet

Moral responsibility does not contract with physical distance or expand with physical proximity. The person who fires a defensive weapon at a distance has made a deliberate choice—assessed a threat, decided to respond, selected a specific action, and accepted its consequences.

Every element of that sequence is fully intentional, fully accountable, and fully subject to the moral evaluation that intentional consequential action always generates.

The physical distance between the person and the outcome of their choice does not interrupt or diminish any part of this moral chain.

The philosopher Jeff McMahan, in his analysis of the ethics of killing, consistently emphasizes that the moral evaluation of lethal action depends upon the relationship between the actor and the threat—upon questions of who initiated the moral crisis, what the defender's relationship to the harm was, and whether the force was necessary and proportionate—rather than upon physical proximity (McMahan, 2009). These are questions about intention, necessity, and moral context. They are not questions about geography.

The Difference Between Distance and Detachment

Physical distance and moral detachment are not the same thing, and treating them as equivalent produces a fundamental error in ethical reasoning. A person can act with extraordinary cruelty at close range—with full physical proximity to the person they are harming—and a person can act with genuine compassion and moral seriousness at considerable distance. What determines the moral character of the act is the mental state, the intention, and the conscience of the actor, not the number of meters separating them from the consequence of their choice.

The Buddhist emphasis on *cetana*—intention as the moral core of action—makes this point with particular clarity. The Stoic tradition's insistence on the governance of action by reason rather than by emotion makes the same point from a different direction. The just war tradition's requirement of right intention as a criterion for legitimate force is another formulation of the same insight. Across traditions that approach the ethics of force from very different theological and philosophical starting points, the consistent conclusion is that moral character resides in consciousness and intention—neither of which is located at a specific physical distance from anything.

Why Firearms Eliminate Physical Disadvantage Rather Than Accountability

What firearms remove from the equation of defensive force is not moral responsibility. It is the requirement that the practical exercise of defensive rights depend upon physical dominance. The elderly person, the physically disabled individual, the person of smaller stature confronting a larger aggressor—these people do not forfeit their moral right to preserve their life simply because they lack the physical capacity to exercise that right through unarmed resistance. The firearm that makes effective defense practically available to them has not diminished their moral accountability for how they use it. It has made it possible for them to exercise moral agency in a situation where physical circumstances would otherwise have rendered them effectively powerless.

This is the moral argument for defensive firearms that the equalizing function of the preceding chapter established—and it applies with particular force to the question of distance. The physically disadvantaged defender who can only establish a meaningful defensive perimeter at distance is not exercising a morally inferior form of defense.

They are exercising the only form of effective defense available to them—and the moral framework that treats this as less legitimate than a form of defense they cannot practically achieve has prioritized physical aesthetics over the actual moral content of what defense is supposed to accomplish.

Why Society Accepts Distance Selectively

Modern societies employ distance as a defensive and protective tool without controversy across a wide range of institutional contexts. Emergency response systems monitor threats remotely. Military forces project defensive capacity over vast geographic ranges. Police use communications, surveillance, and positioning systems that dramatically extend the effective range of protective action.

Deterrence—the prevention of harm through the communicated capacity to respond to it—operates across distances that make the concept of physical proximity essentially irrelevant. The selective discomfort that arises specifically when individual civilians employ distance through firearms reveals that the actual concern is not with distance as such. It is with the distribution of that capability, with who possesses the defensive tools that distance enables, and whether individual citizens should have access to the same practical extension of defensive reach that institutional actors routinely employ.

This is a legitimate policy question. It is not a moral argument about distance. Honest engagement with the ethics of firearms requires acknowledging the difference (Kopel, 1992).

Distance, Judgment, and the Weight of Consequence

Why Effective Defense Requires Greater Moral Seriousness

Firearms do not reduce the moral seriousness of defensive action. They increase it—because they increase the consequences of decision-making errors in both directions. The choice to fire, made incorrectly, produces irreversible harm that a less effective defensive tool might not. The choice not to fire, made incorrectly, may permit irreversible harm that the firearm's greater effectiveness could have prevented.

The increased effectiveness of firearms as defensive tools does not simplify the moral decisions their use requires. It intensifies the demand for the judgment, preparation, and moral clarity that responsible use requires.

This intensification is itself a moral argument, not against firearms but for taking the character formation, training, and disciplined awareness that their responsible possession demands seriously. The person who carries a firearm casually, without having genuinely engaged with the moral weight of what they carry, has not achieved a comfortable moral position by maintaining ignorance. They have failed a responsibility that the capability they possess generates (Grossman, 1995).

The Myth That Physical Struggle Creates Moral Legitimacy

A persistent and largely unexamined assumption in some objections to firearms is the implicit suggestion that defense becomes more ethically authentic when it is physically difficult—that the moral legitimacy of resistance is somehow enhanced by the suffering and physical struggle it involves.

This assumption deserves more critical scrutiny than it typically receives, because it privileges physical hardship as a moral criterion in a way that no serious ethical tradition actually supports.

The traditions examined throughout this book evaluate defensive force according to necessity, proportionality, intention, and restraint. None of them require that defensive force be physically demanding to be morally legitimate.

The morality of defense is determined by what it serves and how it is governed—not by how much physical effort precedes success, and not by how much suffering the defender must absorb before their resistance qualifies as genuine.

A framework that requires defenders to suffer more than necessary in order to satisfy an aesthetic preference for physical authenticity has confused moral symbolism with moral substance—at the expense of the vulnerable people whose effective protection is the actual point.

Why Distance Can Preserve Life Rather Than Cheapen It

The framing of defensive distance as a form of disrespect toward the value of human life inverts the actual moral logic of what distance, in many defensive situations, achieves. Distance may allow a threat to be stopped before prolonged violence has inflicted the injuries that close engagement would produce—before the defender has been seriously harmed, before bystanders have been caught in an escalating confrontation, and before the aggressor has sustained harm beyond what stopping the immediate threat required.

Within the framework of any tradition that takes seriously the obligation to preserve innocent life and minimize harm—the Jewish principle of *pikuach nefesh*, the natural law requirement of proportionality, the Stoic emphasis on necessity—the capacity to achieve these outcomes at a distance is a moral advantage rather than a moral compromise. Distance that enables earlier, less harmful interruption of genuine threat is not a cheapening of the value of human life. It is one of the ways that value can be most effectively honored in practice.

Firearms and the Exposure of Conscience

What many people attribute to moral discomfort with distance is, upon honest examination, often discomfort with the directness of individual moral responsibility that firearms impose. A firearm makes the connection between the person and the consequence of their choice immediate, personal, and impossible to distribute across collective arrangements or institutional structures. It exposes conscience by making evasion unavailable—by requiring the person holding it to make a decision whose moral weight they cannot share or defer to.

This exposure is, philosophically, one of the most significant moral features of individual defensive capability. It is precisely the feature that the traditions of character formation examined throughout this book—Stoic self-command, the Buddhist emphasis on *cetana*, and the Sikh integration of spiritual discipline and defensive readiness—are designed to prepare people for. The discomfort that individual moral responsibility generates when it cannot be evaded is not an argument against that responsibility. It is evidence that the seriousness of what is at stake has been genuinely recognized—and recognition is the beginning, rather than the end, of moral preparation.

Thoughts to Ponder: The Real Measure of Moral Distance

Physical distance and moral distance are fundamentally different concepts, and the conflation of the two has produced more confusion than clarity in discussions of firearms and defensive ethics. Distance has always been a feature of protective action. Moral traditions have never required physical proximity as a criterion for legitimate defense. What they have required—consistently and across traditions separated by centuries and cultures—is intention aligned with protection rather than aggression, force constrained by genuine necessity, and the restraint that prevents defensive action from exceeding the moral purpose that justifies it.

The true measure of moral distance is not how close a defender stands to a threat. It is how closely their actions remain aligned with conscience, responsibility, and the protection of innocent life. A defender who maintains that alignment at close range and a defender who maintains it at distance have both met the standard that serious ethical reasoning demands. What determines moral legitimacy is not geography. It is the character, the judgment, and the disciplined conscience of the person who acts.

Chapter 16:
The Firearm as the Last Resort

Much of the moral anxiety surrounding firearms centers on a specific fear: that possessing a serious defensive tool encourages its use, that preparedness and eagerness are functionally indistinguishable, and that placing a firearm at the end of the defensive continuum is a convenient fiction that the reality of human behavior does not support. This anxiety deserves honest engagement rather than dismissal. The answer that serious ethical analysis produces, however, runs counter to the anxiety's assumptions. Properly understood, the concept of last resort is not a rationalization for casual access to lethal force. It is the moral framework that makes defensive firearms legitimate precisely by restricting them—by defining the narrow conditions under which their use can be justified and insisting upon the exhaustion of every lesser alternative before those conditions are reached.

The Moral Logic of Last Resort

The Historical Role of Last-Resort Force

The principle that force should be employed only when lesser alternatives have genuinely failed is among the oldest and most consistent features of every serious ethical tradition that has engaged with the moral structure of defensive action. The just war tradition's requirement that war be a last resort—that it may be undertaken only when peaceful alternatives have been exhausted—has governed Western moral and legal thinking about force for nearly two millennia.

Natural law reasoning consistently holds that the moral legitimacy of force depends upon its necessity—that force employed when other options remained available has exceeded the moral permission that necessity alone can grant (Aquinas, c. 1265–1274).

The religious traditions examined in preceding chapters reflect the same principle in their own formulations. The Sikh tradition's insistence that the sword be drawn only after peaceful means have failed, the Islamic prohibition against transgression that bounds even justified defensive force, and the Buddhist framework's reluctance toward any action generating harm—these are not identical moral positions, but they share a structural commitment to the same foundational insight: force becomes morally permissible not because it is desirable but because reality sometimes leaves no better alternative.

Why Avoidance Is Morally Preferable Whenever Possible

The moral hierarchy of defensive responses places avoidance, de-escalation, and peaceful resolution above force not merely as practical preferences but as genuine moral priorities. The person who successfully avoids a confrontation—who retreats, escapes, or prevents a situation from escalating to the point where defensive force becomes necessary—has achieved a morally superior outcome to the person who responds with even perfectly proportionate and necessary force. No lives are risked. No harm is inflicted. No moral burden is assumed.

This means that the legitimacy of a last resort depends, at least in part, upon the sincerity with which lesser alternatives were pursued. The person who reaches for a firearm without genuinely considering whether avoidance or de-escalation was possible has not met the moral threshold the last-resort framework requires. The framework demands not only that force be proportionate and necessary at the moment it is employed but also that the person employing it exercise genuine moral discipline in the steps preceding it—arriving at the point of last resort because other options genuinely failed, not because they were never seriously considered (Walzer, 1977).

Why Necessity Creates Moral Permission

Necessity—the genuine absence of adequate alternatives—is the moral threshold that transforms otherwise impermissible force into defensible action. Force employed below this threshold has not met the condition that justifies it. Force employed when danger is imminent, the harm threatened is serious, and no lesser response could adequately address it operates within the moral space that necessity defines.

The last-resort framework does not require that defenders exhaust every conceivable alternative before responding to genuine imminent threat. It requires that they exercise genuine moral discipline in their approach to situations—cultivating habits of avoidance and de-escalation that ensure firearms are reached for only when the moral threshold of necessity has actually been crossed. The discipline is dispositional, cultivated in advance of crisis rather than calculated under pressure in the moment it arrives (Finnis, 1980).

Why Last Resort Is a Moral Category Rather Than a Tactical Preference

The concept of last resort is frequently misunderstood as tactical advice—the practical observation that firearms are most effective when employed as a final escalation after lesser tools have failed. This misreading misses the point.

Last resort is a moral category, not a tactical one. It concerns the ethical sequencing of responses—the hierarchy of values determining which means are appropriate under which conditions.

The moral significance of this distinction is substantial. A person who reaches for a firearm because it is the most effective tool available has not necessarily met the moral threshold the last-resort framework requires. A person who reaches for it because all morally adequate alternatives have genuinely been exhausted has met that threshold—regardless of whether a more effective tool might tactically have been available earlier. The framework disciplines the moral reasoning preceding the decision, not merely the decision itself.

Preparedness Is Not Eagerness

The False Assumption That Possession Equals Desire

Among the more persistent confusions in popular thinking about defensive firearms is the assumption that possessing one indicates willingness, or even desire, to use it, as though the decision to maintain defensive capability reflects an underlying eagerness for the confrontation that capability is designed to address. Genuine preparedness operates according to opposite logic.

The person who has thought seriously about the moral weight of defensive force—who understands what it costs, who has genuinely internalized the traditions of restraint and necessity examined throughout this book—is typically among the least eager to employ it. Awareness of consequence produces reluctance rather than enthusiasm.

The Stoic tradition's emphasis on self-command, the just war tradition's insistence on last resort, the Buddhist framework's understanding of the karmic weight of harmful action—these are not positions producing eagerness for conflict. They produce a profound preference for its avoidance (Aurelius, trans. 2006).

Why Firearms Clarify Moral Boundaries

One of the less frequently acknowledged functions of firearms in the ethical structure of defensive response is their capacity to clarify the moral distinction between ordinary conflict and a genuinely lethal threat. The introduction of a firearm into a defensive calculation is not a minor escalation within a continuous spectrum. It is a categorical shift—from lesser defensive tools and lesser harms to potentially irreversible consequences. This categorical character is itself morally significant.

The gravity that firearms impose upon the decision to employ them reinforces the moral threshold rather than weakening it. A person who understands the full weight of what deploying a firearm means is less likely to reach that decision casually. The seriousness of the tool intensifies the deliberation it requires. Far from encouraging escalation, this seriousness can function as a brake upon it—making unmistakably clear, at every stage of a deteriorating situation, how consequential the decision to escalate to the final resort actually is (McMahan, 2009).

Escalation, Intention, and Human Agency

Conflict escalates because of human choices—because aggression advances, because judgment fails, because ego supersedes conscience, because malicious intent finds opportunity.

It does not escalate because tools of serious consequence exist in the vicinity of conflict. The person who escalates a confrontation to the point where lethal force becomes genuinely necessary has made a series of moral choices that the mere existence of defensive capability did not determine.

This matters because the alternative framing—that defensive firearms encourage escalation by their presence—mislocates moral agency in the tool rather than in the human beings whose choices actually govern what occurs. The traditions examined throughout this book are united on this point: moral responsibility resides in persons, not instruments. Addressing the failure of restraint that produces escalation requires attention to human character and moral formation, not to the presence of tools whose moral character depends entirely upon those who govern them.

The Difference Between Escalation and Resolution

The last resort, properly employed, does not extend conflict. It terminates it. The defensive use of a firearm is oriented not toward the continuation of confrontation but toward its immediate resolution—toward stopping the specific harm that has made its use necessary and ceasing force at the moment that purpose has been achieved. This orientation distinguishes last-resort defensive force from every morally disqualifying alternative: retaliation, which extends conflict backward toward a prior injury; punishment, which extends it forward toward a desired consequence; and domination, which extends it outward toward a broader assertion of power.

The person who employs a firearm as a genuine last resort is not seeking to win a conflict. They are seeking to end one, specifically, the one that the aggressor's conduct has made necessary.

Deterrence, Maturity, and the Ethics of Final Boundaries

Why Deterrence Matters Morally

The most successful employment of a last resort may be the one that never occurs—the confrontation abandoned because the potential aggressor perceived that it would encounter a genuinely capable defensive response. A clearly understood and credible final boundary can prevent the escalation that would otherwise make its exercise necessary.

This preventive function of last-resort capability is not merely tactical. It is a moral one—perhaps the most significant moral benefit that genuine defensive preparedness produces. The harm that never occurs because adequate defensive capability was present and understood is as real, in moral terms, as the harm stopped after it had begun. A moral framework for firearms acknowledging only the latter and ignoring the former has not engaged honestly with the full range of morally significant outcomes that defensive capability actually produces (Kleck, 1997).

Firearms as Tools of Serious Consequence

The irreversibility of firearms' effects is not incidental to their moral significance. It is central to it. The decision to employ a firearm in a defensive situation cannot be undone. This finality places a specific moral demand upon those who bear defensive firearms—a demand for the deliberation, maturity, and genuine moral preparedness that decisions of irreversible consequence require.

The person who carries a firearm without having thought seriously about what employing it actually means has accepted a responsibility without accepting its full scope. The traditions of character formation running through this book—Stoic self-mastery, the Hindu emphasis on *svadharma*, the Sikh integration of spiritual discipline and defensive readiness—all understand that genuine capability requires genuine preparation, and that preparation must be moral as well as technical. The seriousness of the consequence narrows the legitimate range of the decision rather than expanding it.

Why Last Resorts Require Character More Than Capability

Technical capacity to operate a firearm effectively is, within the moral framework of last resort, necessary but insufficient. Technical skill determines whether defensive action is effective. Character determines whether it is right—whether the threshold of genuine necessity was actually met, whether the commitment to exhaust lesser alternatives was genuinely honored, and whether the force employed remained bounded by proportionality and terminated at the moment necessity ceased.

These are not questions that technical training answers. They are questions that moral formation addresses through the cultivation of patience, humility, emotional discipline, and genuine commitment to the avoidance that serious defensive ethics requires. The person of outstanding technical skill who lacks this moral formation is more dangerous than the person of lesser skill who possesses it. Capability without character is not preparedness. It is a different kind of risk (Grossman, 1995).

The Last Resort as a Safeguard Against Vigilantism

The last-resort framework serves an important function in distinguishing legitimate defensive force from vigilantism. The vigilante does not approach force as a last resort. They approach it as a preferred tool—one they actively seek occasions to employ, one that satisfies rather than burdens them. The last-resort framework is structurally incompatible with this orientation. It requires reluctance rather than eagerness, avoidance rather than confrontation, and the genuine exhaustion of peaceful alternatives rather than the performance of consideration followed by the predetermined conclusion that force was necessary.

The responsible defender approaches every potential confrontation with the explicit goal of not reaching the point at which last-resort force becomes necessary. They retreat when retreat is available. They de-escalate when de-escalation is possible. This orientation—reluctant, disciplined, genuinely committed to avoidance—is both the moral mark of the last-resort framework and its practical safeguard against the corruption that eagerness for force invariably produces.

Thoughts to Ponder: The Boundary That Ends Force

The moral legitimacy of firearms as defensive tools does not reside in their effectiveness alone. It resides in their disciplined placement at the end of the defensive continuum—in their role as the final boundary protecting innocent life when all lesser responses have genuinely failed. That placement is not merely a practical description of how firearms are most effectively used.

It is the moral structure within which their use can be justified at all.

Preparedness differs fundamentally from eagerness. The person who has genuinely internalized the last-resort framework is not anticipating the opportunity to employ force. They are a person who has accepted the burden of maintaining a final boundary—carrying that burden with the seriousness, reluctance, and moral gravity that genuine responsibility requires—and who regards the confrontation they never have to face as the measure of their success rather than its absence.

The next chapter addresses a question that follows directly from this framework: if misuse of firearms exists—and it does—does that misuse invalidate their legitimate defensive function, or does moral seriousness require the careful distinction between abuse and proper use that every serious ethical tradition applies to every other domain of human capability?

Chapter 17:

Misuse vs. Moral Legitimacy

One of the most emotionally compelling arguments against firearms ownership takes the following form: firearms are sometimes used to commit terrible harm; therefore, the moral legitimacy of civilian firearms ownership is questionable at best and indefensible at worst. The appeal of this argument is genuine.

Harm draws attention to the instrument involved, and the instrument's association with that harm lingers in ways that make dispassionate analysis difficult. But emotional resonance and logical validity are not the same thing—and the argument from misuse, examined carefully, commits a fundamental error in moral reasoning: it treats abuse as evidence against legitimate use rather than as a violation of the standards that legitimate use defines.

Why Misuse Does Not Determine Moral Legitimacy

The Difference Between Use and Abuse

The concept of misuse presupposes the existence of proper use. This is not a semantic observation. It is a structural one with direct implications for the argument being examined. When we say that a firearm has been misused, we are implicitly invoking a standard of correct use against which the misuse is being measured.

The abuse is identifiable as abuse precisely because it violates the conditions—necessity, proportionality, restraint, defensive intent—that legitimate use requires. Without those conditions, without the standard of proper use against which violations can be assessed, the concept of misuse becomes incoherent.

This means that the argument from misuse actually depends upon the existence of legitimate use for its own coherence. To argue that misuse invalidates the legitimacy of firearms ownership is to saw off the branch upon which the argument sits—to eliminate the standard without which "misuse" cannot even be meaningfully defined.

Human moral reasoning has consistently recognized this structure across every domain in which the possibility of misuse arises. The misuse of authority does not invalidate authority.

The misuse of medicine does not eliminate the legitimacy of medical practice. The misuse of speech does not dissolve the moral case for free expression (Mill, 1859). In each case, the response to abuse is the articulation and enforcement of standards governing proper use—not the conclusion that use itself is illegitimate.

Why Power Always Carries Risk

The possibility of misuse is not a distinctive feature of firearms that marks them out for special moral suspicion. It is a feature of every meaningful form of human capability. Physical strength can be exercised protectively or predatorily. Legal authority can serve justice or oppression. Wealth can support human flourishing or corrupt it. Technology can extend human capacity for good or amplify human capacity for harm. Speech can inform and enlighten or manipulate and destroy. Political influence can protect democratic institutions or undermine them.

The philosopher John Stuart Mill's observation that the capacity for harm is inseparable from the capacity for significant good is among the most consistent insights in the history of moral thought (Mill, 1859). Power without the possibility of misuse is not meaningful power—it is capability so constrained that it cannot produce significant consequences in either direction.

The response of morally serious societies to this reality is not to eliminate capability but to develop the governance structures—training, accountability, regulation, discipline, moral formation—that make its responsible exercise more likely and its abuse more detectable and consequential.

Medicine, Transportation, and Other Analogies

The consistency with which moral reasoning applies across analogous cases is one of its most important tests. Consider the moral logic that governs responses to misuse in other domains involving serious capability.

Medical practitioners possess the knowledge to harm as well as to heal—and the response to medical malpractice is not the elimination of medicine but the development of training standards, licensing requirements, accountability structures, and professional ethics that govern the exercise of medical capability (Beauchamp & Childress, 2019).

Automobiles cause tens of thousands of deaths annually—and the response is driver education, licensing, traffic regulation, and safety standards rather than the conclusion that motorized transport is morally illegitimate.

The principle is consistent: Where significant capability exists alongside significant potential for misuse, the morally serious response is governance rather than elimination—the development of the standards, structures, and character formation that make responsible use the norm and hold misuse to appropriate account. The question that moral consistency demands is whether this principle applies equally to firearms.

Arguments for categorical exceptionalism—for treating firearms as uniquely subject to a standard of zero-tolerance for misuse that no other form of human capability is held to—carry the burden of explaining why the principle that applies everywhere else should not apply here.

Why Misuse Alone Cannot Serve as a Universal Moral Standard

The standard implied by the argument from misuse—that the presence of abuse disqualifies the legitimacy of the thing abused—cannot be applied consistently without eliminating virtually every institution and capability that human civilization depends upon.

Law is misused by corrupt officials and unjust systems. Democratic processes are misused by demagogues and manipulators. Religion is misused to justify oppression and violence. Education is misused to indoctrinate rather than to develop genuine understanding.

No serious moral thinker concludes from these observations that law, democracy, religion, or education are therefore morally illegitimate. The conclusion they draw is that these institutions must be governed by the ethical standards that distinguish proper use from abuse—and that the existence of abuse confirms rather than dissolves the need for those standards. The same reasoning applies to firearms. Misuse confirms the need for moral governance. It does not establish the absence of legitimate use (Walzer, 1977).

Moral Agency, Responsibility, and the Location of Blame

Why Human Choice Remains Central

Every tradition of moral philosophy examined in this book returns, ultimately, to the same foundational conviction: that moral responsibility resides in persons rather than instruments. Tools possess no intention, no judgment, no conscience, no capacity for restraint or excess. Human beings provide all of these—the purpose, the deliberation, the motivation, and the moral governance or its absence that determines the character of what occurs.

This means that the primary object of moral evaluation in any situation involving the use of a tool is the human agent who employed it—their intentions, their judgment, the moral formation that shaped their decision-making, and the accountability they bear for the consequences of their choices. Aristotle's foundational account of moral responsibility places voluntary choice at the center of ethical evaluation—the act is what it is because of the agent who chose it, not because of the instrument through which it was expressed (Aristotle, trans. 2009). This insight has survived two and a half millennia of philosophical scrutiny because it reflects something accurate and important about the structure of moral life.

The Temptation of Instrumental Blame

The desire to assign blame to instruments rather than to persons is psychologically understandable even when it is philosophically indefensible. Instruments cannot argue back. They cannot claim mitigating circumstances.

They cannot invoke the complexity of their intentions or the difficulty of their situation. They sit as silent, concrete, uncomplicated objects that seem to offer a clear and manageable focal point for moral concern.

The human beings whose choices actually determined the outcome are complex, embedded in circumstances, and resistant to the clean causal narratives that emotional processing under conditions of grief and anger tends to prefer.

The philosopher Hannah Arendt, in her examination of how moral responsibility functions within complex systems of action, observed that the diffusion of responsibility—the displacement of moral accounting away from specific human choices toward abstract causes, systems, or instruments—is among the most consistent failures of ethical reasoning under pressure (Arendt, 1963).

Blaming the tool provides emotional relief from the more demanding work of understanding the human failures—of character, of moral formation, of social and institutional conditions—that actually produced the outcome. It appears to offer a solution while systematically avoiding engagement with the problem.

Why Denying Agency Weakens Accountability

The practical consequence of instrumental blame is the weakening of precisely the accountability structures that genuine moral seriousness requires. If wrongdoing is attributed primarily to the presence of tools rather than to the choices of moral agents, the logical implication is that removing the tools addresses the problem, and the human beings whose choices, character, and conditions actually generated the harm escape the scrutiny they deserve.

This displacement of accountability does not only fail to address the underlying problem. It actively undermines the moral framework upon which genuine accountability depends.

A society that attributes harmful action primarily to the instruments through which it was expressed has, in effect, denied the moral agency of the person who made the choices that mattered. And the denial of agency is not a morally neutral position. It is the erosion of the foundational assumption—that human beings are responsible for their choices and accountable for their consequences—upon which ethical life depends (McMahan, 2009).

Firearms as Amplifiers Rather Than Creators of Agency

The morally significant feature of firearms is not that they introduce harmful intention into human experience—harmful intention preceded them by the full length of recorded history. It is that they amplify the consequences of the intentions already present in the persons who employ them. The harmful intention finds a more effective means of expression. The protective intention finds a more effective means of exercise. The reckless judgment produces more severe consequences. The disciplined judgment produces more effective results.

This amplification increases the moral weight of the choices made by those who bear firearms—it raises the stakes of judgment, the consequences of recklessness, and the importance of the character formation that responsible use requires. What it does not do is replace human agency with mechanical causation or exempt the person making choices from accountability for the choices they make. The seriousness of firearms strengthens the case for accountability. It does not provide a substitute for it.

Governance, Stewardship, and the Moral Response to Misuse

Why Serious Tools Demand Serious Stewardship

The appropriate moral response to the existence of misuse in any domain of significant capability is not the abandonment of that capability but the development of the governance structures, training standards, and character formation that make responsible use more likely and abuse more detectable and consequential. This principle applies with particular force where the consequences of misuse are severe, because the severity of potential consequences increases the moral obligation of governance rather than arguing for the elimination of the capability itself.

Firearms ownership, within this framework, carries with it a specific and demanding set of obligations: to training, to the development of sound judgment, to the emotional discipline that prevents capability from being governed by the reactive states that threatening situations generate, and to the ongoing accountability that serious stewardship requires. These are not obligations that diminish over time or that can be discharged by the initial decision to possess responsibly. They are continuous, as continuous as the capability itself (Grossman, 1995).

The Invisible Side of Defensive Capability

The moral accounting of firearms legitimacy is systematically distorted by a visibility asymmetry that honest ethical reasoning must acknowledge and correct. The harms that firearms inflict when misused are documented, reported, analyzed, and publicly mourned—as they should be.

They are visible in the most literal sense: they leave behind evidence, records, and the unmistakable presence of genuine suffering.

The harms that firearms prevent when used defensively or as deterrents are largely invisible. The assault that did not occur, the intrusion abandoned when defensive capability was perceived, the escalation that never happened because a clear boundary existed—these outcomes leave no crime reports, no medical records, and no news coverage.

The researcher Gary Kleck, whose empirical work on defensive gun use remains among the most carefully conducted in the field, documented the scale of this invisible side of the moral ledger—finding that defensive uses of firearms occur with a frequency that the visible record of violence, focused exclusively on harm inflicted, systematically obscures (Kleck, 1997). Honest moral evaluation of firearms cannot restrict itself to one side of this ledger.

Why Moral Frameworks Distinguish Use From Abuse

The recurring principles that have structured the ethical framework of this book—necessity, proportionality, restraint, accountability, and defensive intent—are not arbitrary preferences.

They are the moral standards that distinguish legitimate use from abuse across every tradition that has addressed the ethics of force seriously. Their function is precisely to provide the criteria against which particular uses of defensive capability can be assessed—criteria that identify abuse as abuse and legitimate use as legitimate use with the precision that moral reasoning requires.

Misuse of firearms—use that is not genuinely necessary, not proportionate, not oriented toward protection rather than aggression, not bounded by the restraint that moral legitimacy demands—violates these standards. That violation confirms the need for the standards rather than undermining their validity.

A moral framework that responds to the violation of its principles by abandoning those principles has not achieved greater consistency. It has abandoned the possibility of moral reasoning about the domain in question altogether.

Firearms Ownership as a Test of Ethical Maturity

The moral challenge that firearms ownership presents is, ultimately, a challenge of ethical maturity—the capacity to accept significant capability alongside the full weight of the responsibility that capability generates without retreating into either the recklessness that ignores consequence or the evasion of responsibility that transfers it elsewhere.

Ownership is not entitlement. It is stewardship—the acceptance of an ongoing obligation toward judgment, discipline, and accountability that does not diminish with familiarity or comfort.

The traditions examined throughout this book—the Stoic emphasis on self-command, the just war tradition's insistence on restraint, the Jewish framework's understanding that capability generates obligation, the Sikh integration of spiritual discipline and defensive readiness—all converge on the same foundational insight: the answer to the possibility of misuse is not the abandonment of capability but the deepening of the commitment to govern it responsibly. That commitment, sustained with genuine seriousness and genuine humility, is what transforms possession from a mere fact about a person into a moral achievement.

Thoughts to Ponder: Responsibility in an Imperfect World

Misuse and moral legitimacy occupy different categories. The existence of the first does not determine the absence of the second—any more than the existence of medical malpractice determines the illegitimacy of medicine, or the existence of judicial corruption determines the illegitimacy of law. What the existence of misuse determines is the necessity of the governance, accountability, and moral formation without which any significant human capability tends toward abuse.

To reject all legitimate use because misuse exists is to reject the concept of moral agency itself—to conclude that because human beings sometimes exercise capability badly, the possibility of exercising it well should be eliminated rather than cultivated. Ethical life depends upon the opposite conviction: that human beings can be held responsible for how they exercise power, that the standards distinguishing proper use from abuse are real and meaningful, and that the appropriate response to their violation is accountability rather than the abandonment of the moral framework that makes accountability possible.

Part V

The Informed Perspective

(Chapters 18-23)

From everyone who has been given much, much will be demanded; and from the one who has been entrusted with much, much more will be asked.
— Luke 12:48

Chapter 18:

Disarming the Innocent Is Not Moral Progress

Few moral impulses are more understandable than the desire to reduce harm by reducing access to the tools through which harm is inflicted.

The aspiration is genuine, the concern legitimate, and anyone who has encountered the consequences of violence knows that the impulse toward prevention deserves serious moral respect rather than dismissal.

The problem is not the aspiration.

The problem is the assumption embedded within it—that restricting defensive capability is equivalent to reducing danger, and that good intentions directed at a serious problem are sufficient to establish the moral legitimacy of the policy they motivate.

Moral reasoning that evaluates outcomes as well as intentions cannot accept this equivalence.

The question ethical analysis must ask is not only what a policy intends but also what it actually produces—and specifically, who bears the consequences when outcomes diverge from the intentions that generated them.

Disarmament and the Redistribution of Vulnerability

Why Power Does Not Disappear When Tools Are Removed

The moral case for restricting defensive firearms capability rests, at least implicitly, upon the premise that doing so reduces the overall power available for violence.

This premise is more intuitive than accurate. Aggressive intent does not disappear when tools most commonly used to express it become less accessible to law-abiding individuals.

It persists—and often finds alternative means of expression, or simply encounters less organized opposition from those whose defensive capability has been reduced.

The moral philosopher Michael Huemer observes that the most consistent pattern in the study of restrictions on defensive capability is not the elimination of violence but its redistribution—the shift in practical power between those willing to violate legal and moral norms to obtain capability and those unwilling to do so (Huemer, 2012).

Aggression is, at its core, a willingness to operate outside moral and legal constraints.

Policies that apply most reliably to those who operate within constraints produce, as their practical consequence, a widening gap between the capability available to aggressors and the capability available to those they target.

The Difference Between Disarming Aggressors and Disarming the Innocent

The ethical evaluation of any policy restricting defensive capability depends substantially on who actually bears the burden of compliance. People already committed to operating within moral and legal norms comply with restrictions more reliably than those already committed to violating them. A restriction applying most reliably to the former produces, as its primary effect, the reduction of defensive capability among precisely those people whose use of that capability was already governed by moral restraint and legal compliance.

John Lott's empirical analysis documents this asymmetry, finding that restrictions on defensive capability tend to affect law-abiding individuals more reliably than those whose conduct already places them outside legal constraint (Lott, 2000). This is not a technical policy observation that can be set aside as irrelevant to moral analysis. It is a direct description of who absorbs the moral costs of the policy in question—and any ethical framework evaluating policies solely by intention rather than by distribution of consequence has not completed its moral analysis.

Why Vulnerability Carries Moral Weight

Vulnerability is not a morally neutral condition. It is a condition with real consequences—exposure to harm, the inability to protect those in one's care, and genuine helplessness in situations where capability might have made a decisive difference.

The moral traditions examined throughout this book have consistently treated the protection of innocent life as a foundational obligation precisely because they take seriously what the vulnerability of innocent life actually costs.

When a policy increases the vulnerability of people who have done nothing to warrant increased exposure to harm—who have complied with every legal and moral requirement placed upon them—the moral costs of that increased vulnerability do not disappear because the policy was motivated by good intentions.

They fall upon the people who experience them, with the full weight that genuine vulnerability carries (Kleck, 1997).

The Historical Reality of Opportunistic Aggression

The historical record provides consistent evidence for a principle that moral systems cannot afford to ignore: predatory behavior responds primarily to opportunity rather than aspiration.

The aggressor who confronts meaningful resistance encounters a cost that affects their calculation in ways that moral condemnation alone does not. The aggressor who encounters no meaningful resistance faces a correspondingly reduced practical obstacle to whatever harm they intend (Keeley, 1996).

Moral frameworks constructed upon the assumption that the expression of good values will reliably produce corresponding behavioral changes in those committed to predation have consistently failed the populations they were designed to protect.

Taking seriously the reality of opportunistic aggression is not cynicism. It is the beginning of moral reasoning adequate to the world that actually exists.

Dependency, Protection, and the Limits of Institutions

Why Institutions Matter

Nothing in this chapter's argument constitutes a case against the institutions of law enforcement, judicial authority, and organized public safety that constitute the first and most important line of protection in any functioning civil society. These institutions represent genuine moral achievements—the organized expression of the community's collective commitment to protecting its members from predatory harm. Their importance is real, and the argument that follows does not diminish it.

What the argument addresses is the assumption that institutional protection is so comprehensive and reliable that individual defensive capability becomes genuinely redundant. This assumption is not accurate, and its inaccuracy has moral consequences that honest ethical reasoning cannot avoid.

The Limits of Institutional Protection

Law enforcement operates under constraints of geography, response time, resource allocation, and human fallibility that no institutional excellence can entirely eliminate. The gap between when violence begins and when institutional response arrives is not a marginal exception to a generally reliable system. It is a structural feature of every institutional protective arrangement that has ever existed. In rural areas, response times are extended by geography. In urban areas, resource constraints affect availability. In crisis conditions—natural disasters, civil unrest, and system failures—institutional protection can become unavailable precisely when the conditions producing danger are most acute. David Kopel's comparative analysis documents the consistency with which institutional protection gaps create situations in which individuals facing genuine imminent threat have no realistic access to the assistance institutional protection is designed to provide (Kopel, 1992).

A moral framework evaluating defensive capability solely under conditions of reliable institutional availability has not engaged with the full range of situations in which the moral question of self-defense becomes practically urgent.

Who Bears the Risk When Protection Fails?

The experience of institutional failure is distributed as unevenly as institutional protection itself. When law enforcement response is delayed, when geographical isolation makes timely intervention impossible, when crisis conditions disrupt normal protective functioning, the individuals who bear the consequences are not those with resources to purchase supplementary private protection or to arrange their lives in ways that minimize exposure to the gap between institutional aspiration and institutional reality.

They are ordinary people—families in isolated areas, individuals in under-resourced communities—whose economic circumstances leave them dependent upon the institutional protection that is, in moments of genuine crisis, unavailable.

The moral weight of this distribution of risk is central to the ethical evaluation of policies increasing individual vulnerability.

The abstract discussion of disarmament as moral progress becomes considerably more concrete when understood in terms of the specific populations upon whom increased vulnerability is most likely to be concentrated (Lott, 2000).

Dependency as a Moral Condition

Dependency is not inherently problematic. Human beings are social creatures whose flourishing depends upon networks of mutual reliance that no individual can replicate through self-sufficiency alone. The issue is not dependency as such but the moral conditions under which it is imposed.

When a policy removes the practical option of individual defensive capability and substitutes reliance upon institutional protection whose reliability is uneven and whose availability in moments of genuine crisis cannot be guaranteed, the people affected have not been protected. They have been made more dependent upon a system that may or may not be present when the protection it is supposed to provide becomes necessary (Huemer, 2012). A society should carefully justify any policy that increases involuntary vulnerability without providing reliable substitute protection.

Moral Equality, Justice, and Defensive Capability

The Principle of Equal Human Worth

The traditions examined throughout this book converge on a foundational conviction: every person possesses equal moral worth that places upon those capable of protecting them an obligation of corresponding seriousness. If every human life genuinely possesses this worth, then the question of how effectively innocent life is protected cannot be a matter of secondary concern. Equal moral worth implies equal moral seriousness about the practical conditions that determine whether that worth can be defended against unjust attack. The value assigned to human life should influence the seriousness with which the practical means of its protection are approached (Finnis, 1980).

Why Capability and Equality Are Connected

The gap between the formal affirmation of equal human worth and the practical distribution of defensive capability is not morally neutral. People with significant economic resources retain access to protective options—private security, secure residential arrangements, geographic insulation—that are not available to those without comparable resources. The restriction of individual defensive capability does not eliminate this gap. It widens it by removing one of the few means through which people without supplementary private protection could meaningfully compensate for the unevenness of institutional coverage.

A system in which those with resources maintain effective defensive capability through private arrangements, while those without resources are left increasingly dependent upon institutional protection whose gaps they are least equipped to absorb, has not achieved moral equality. It has institutionalized a moral inequality in which the practical protection of human life is distributed according to economic circumstance rather than according to the equal moral worth that every serious ethical tradition affirms (McMahan, 2009).

The Difference Between Safety and Dependency

Genuine safety and imposed dependency are not the same condition. Safety is a condition in which individuals and communities possess the resilience and capability to navigate genuine threats with reasonable confidence.

Dependency is a condition in which individuals have been made reliant upon external protection they can neither supplement nor replace when that provision fails.

A morally healthy society pursues genuine safety—building institutional protective capacity while also supporting individual capability, responsibility, and moral formation that genuine resilience requires.

These two dimensions are not in competition. They are complementary expressions of the same commitment to the serious protection of human life that equal moral worth demands. The pretense that institutional protection alone can provide that seriousness, and that individual defensive capability is therefore morally suspect, has not achieved a higher form of protection. It has achieved a comfortable illusion at the expense of the people whose safety it was supposed to serve.

Defensive Capacity as a Component of Moral Agency

Throughout this book, the traditions of moral philosophy and religious ethics examined have consistently converged on a single foundational insight: moral responsibility requires not only good intentions but also the practical capacity to act upon them. The person who accepts the obligation to protect those in their care must also accept the responsibility to ensure they possess the capability to fulfill it when genuine threat arrives.

Removing defensive capability from morally responsible individuals does not remove their moral obligations. It removes their capacity to discharge those obligations effectively. The parent who cannot protect their child has not been relieved of the responsibility to do so. They have been left with the obligation and denied the means—a condition that imposes the full moral weight of responsibility alongside the practical helplessness of incapacity. A moral framework that produces this condition and calls it progress has confused the appearance of virtue with its substance.

Thoughts to Ponder: Progress or Abdication?

Genuine moral progress in the domain of defensive ethics is not measured by the visibility of restraint imposed upon the innocent. It is measured by the effectiveness with which innocent life is actually protected—by the degree to which moral agents possess the capability, the formation, and the institutional support needed to fulfill the obligations that the equal worth of human life generates.

Disarmament that removes defensive capability from people who have done nothing to forfeit it, that increases the vulnerability of those least able to absorb it, and that widens the gap between those with resources to maintain protective alternatives and those without—does not advance this measure of moral progress. It redistributes danger downward, concentrating it among ordinary people in the moments when institutional protection is most absent, while offering the consolation of good intentions to those whose safety is least affected by the consequences of the policy they support.

True moral progress equips moral agents to act responsibly under threat. It takes seriously the practical conditions under which innocent life can be protected. And it refuses the comfortable substitution of symbolic restraint for the genuine protection of human dignity that equal moral worth demands.

Chapter 19:

Responsibility as the Moral Gatekeeper

The language of rights dominates contemporary discussions of firearms ownership in ways that, while legally important, are philosophically incomplete. Rights describe what is permitted. They establish the boundaries within which individuals may act without interference from others or from the state. What they do not establish, by themselves, is whether any particular exercise of those rights is morally serious, ethically prepared, or genuinely worthy of the moral legitimacy that rights language tends to confer.

That determination belongs to responsibility—and responsibility, within any coherent moral framework, is not a qualification appended reluctantly to rights discourse. It is the condition without which rights become entitlement, and entitlement becomes the corruption of moral agency rather than its expression.

Why Rights Require Responsibilities

The Moral Structure of Rights and Duties

The claim that meaningful rights carry corresponding obligations is not a novel philosophical position. It is among the most consistent features of every serious moral tradition that has engaged with the relationship between freedom and accountability.

John Stuart Mill's foundational treatment of liberty established that the freedom of each person is necessarily bounded by the obligation not to harm others—that rights are not unlimited claims but structured permissions whose exercise is governed by corresponding duties toward the community within which they are exercised (Mill, 1859).

This structure appears across the full range of rights that serious moral traditions have recognized. The freedom of speech carries the obligation of truthfulness and the responsibility to distinguish persuasion from manipulation. Political authority carries the obligation of justice toward those over whom it is exercised. Property carries the obligation of stewardship—the recognition that possessing resources confers responsibility for how they are used rather than a license for their arbitrary disposal. The right of self-defense carries the obligation of restraint—the insistence that defensive capability be governed by necessity, proportionality, and the moral seriousness that genuine protective action requires.

In each case, the right and the responsibility are not separate elements that happen to coexist. They are structurally connected—the responsibility defining the moral conditions under which the right can be legitimately exercised and the right losing its moral character when those conditions are not met. A society that values rights while neglecting responsibilities does not achieve greater freedom. It achieves a moral environment in which entitlement displaces accountability, and the discipline that makes rights coherent gradually dissolves.

Why Capacity Increases Obligation

The relationship between capability and moral obligation is among the most consistent patterns in the history of ethical thought.

The Stoic tradition's insistence on self-command as the foundation of virtuous action, the just war tradition's requirement that force be governed by proportionality and restraint, and the Hindu framework's understanding that *svadharma*—specific duty—increases with capability and role all reflect the same underlying moral logic: that the possession of significant capability places the one who possesses it in a different moral relationship to the situations in which that capability becomes relevant (Hadot, 1998).

This is not an intuition unique to any single tradition. It reflects the accurate recognition that consequence and responsibility are structurally connected—that the ability to produce significant outcomes, positive or negative, generates a corresponding obligation to exercise the judgment, discipline, and moral seriousness that the significance of those outcomes requires. Capability does not excuse the person who possesses it from the demands of moral governance. It intensifies those demands in direct proportion to the severity of the consequences that irresponsible exercise could produce.

Why Firearms Intensify the Relationship Between Right and Duty

Firearms magnify the consequences of decision-making with a speed and severity that most other instruments of human capability cannot match. The decision to employ defensive force with a firearm produces outcomes that are immediate, severe, and largely irreversible.

This irreversibility is not incidental to the moral framework governing responsible ownership. It is the feature that most directly intensifies the obligation toward preparation, judgment, and restraint that the right of defensive ownership generates. The person who treats firearms ownership as a right requiring no corresponding moral preparation has misunderstood the structure of the right they are claiming. They have accepted the permission without accepting the obligation—and without the obligation, the permission loses its moral character.

The legitimacy of firearms ownership depends not upon the legal recognition of the right but upon the willingness to accept, with full seriousness, the corresponding duties that meaningful capability generates (McMahan, 2009).

Why Entitlement Corrodes Moral Legitimacy

The most significant moral danger in rights discourse divorced from responsibility is not the external harm that irresponsible exercise of those rights may produce, though that harm is real and serious. It is the internal corruption of the moral agent who has come to regard their rights as entitlements rather than as structured permissions carrying genuine obligations.

Entitlement—the belief that one's rights exist independent of corresponding responsibilities toward others and toward the moral order within which those rights are exercised—is not a stronger form of freedom. It is the degradation of freedom into self-centeredness.

The political philosopher Edmund Burke's observation that liberty, detached from duty and discipline, degrades into license captures this dynamic with enduring precision (Burke, 1790).

Applied to firearms ownership, this means that the person who approaches their defensive capability as an entitlement—who is unwilling to accept the training, the emotional discipline, the restraint, and the ongoing accountability that responsible ownership requires—has not achieved a fuller expression of their rights. They have abandoned the moral framework that makes those rights coherent, replacing moral agency with the appearance of it.

The Internal Gatekeeper: Character Before Crisis

Why Ethical Decisions Cannot Be Improvised

Crisis does not create character. It reveals it. The decisions made in the compressed, emotionally charged, information-poor conditions of a genuine defensive emergency are not made from scratch in the moment they are required. They are made from the habits, dispositions, and moral commitments that have been cultivated—or neglected—in the ordinary conditions that precede the crisis. The person who has not engaged seriously with the moral questions surrounding their defensive capability before crisis arrives will not suddenly become capable of engaging with them under conditions specifically designed to make clear thinking as difficult as possible.

This is why the traditions of moral formation examined throughout this book place such consistent emphasis on preparation—not merely technical preparation but the prior moral reflection that determines how capability will be governed when the conditions governing its use are least favorable to deliberation. The Stoic practice of *premeditatio malorum*—the deliberate advance contemplation of difficult circumstances—was not morbid speculation. It was practical moral preparation: the cultivation, in conditions of calm, of the dispositions and judgments that would be required in conditions of pressure (Aurelius, trans. 2006).

The questions that genuine moral preparation for firearms ownership requires are specific and demanding: Why am I maintaining this capability? What am I protecting, and why does it matter?

Under what conditions would I actually employ force, and under what conditions would I not? What limits govern my actions, and have I genuinely internalized those limits or merely acknowledged them? The time to establish honest answers to these questions is not during a defensive emergency. It is long before one.

Why Responsibility Extends Beyond Legal Compliance

Law establishes the minimum moral threshold—the floor beneath which conduct becomes legally impermissible. It does not establish the ceiling of what moral seriousness requires.

The space between legal compliance and genuine moral responsibility is substantial, and firearms ownership occupies it in ways that demand honest engagement rather than the comfortable assumption that meeting legal requirements has discharged the full scope of moral obligation.

Legal compliance permits negligence that does not rise to the criminal threshold. It permits recklessness that produces harm without satisfying the legal standards for criminal liability. It permits indifference toward the moral weight of capability that falls short of actionable legal failure while representing genuine ethical inadequacy.

Conscience, within the framework that every serious moral tradition examined in this book has affirmed, remains morally relevant even in spaces where law is silent—and the person whose moral preparation extends only to the boundary of legal requirement has not achieved moral seriousness.

They have achieved legal compliance, which is a significantly different and significantly lesser thing (Finnis, 1980).

Training as Moral Formation

The technical dimensions of firearms training—proficiency with the specific instrument, accuracy under various conditions, and familiarity with mechanical function—are necessary components of responsible ownership but not sufficient ones. Technical proficiency determines whether a defensive action is effective. It does not determine whether it was right—whether the threshold of genuine necessity was met, whether the force employed was proportionate, or whether the commitment to exhaust lesser alternatives was genuinely honored.

These determinations depend upon a different kind of preparation: the development of situational awareness, the cultivation of emotional regulation under stress, and the formation of the judgment that distinguishes genuine defensive necessity from situations that require a different response. Dave Grossman's research on the psychological dimensions of lethal decision-making establishes that training that addresses only technical proficiency leaves the practitioner unprepared for the most demanding aspects of genuine defensive responsibility—the aspects that determine moral quality rather than tactical effectiveness (Grossman, 1995). The disciplined mind is the precondition for the disciplined hand—and the formation of the disciplined mind requires deliberate moral education alongside technical training.

Humility as a Requirement of Responsibility

The traditions examined throughout this book converge on a feature of genuine moral seriousness that is easily overlooked in popular discussions of defensive capability: humility. The person who has genuinely engaged with the moral weight of defensive force—who understands what it costs, who has honestly assessed the possibility of error under pressure, and who carries the responsibility of capability without the comfort of certainty about their own infallibility—is less likely to approach situations of potential conflict with bravado than the person whose engagement with these questions has been superficial.

This humility is not weakness. It is the epistemically accurate response to the genuine uncertainty that attends all moral decision-making under pressure. The Stoic practitioner who understood the limits of their own judgment; the Buddhist practitioner who maintained awareness of the mental states that could corrupt their intentions; the just war thinker who insisted upon the last-resort principle precisely because they recognized the human tendency toward rationalization—all were expressing, in their specific idioms, the same foundational insight: that the awareness of fallibility is a feature of moral seriousness rather than its absence (Robertson, 2019).

Responsibility, Trust, and Moral Stewardship

Why Trust Depends Upon Conduct

Moral authority in the domain of defensive capability is not established by assertion. It is demonstrated through conduct—through the consistent exercise of the judgment, restraint, and accountability that responsible ownership requires, sustained over time and across the full range of situations in which capability and restraint interact.

Public trust in the moral legitimacy of civilian defensive capability is not produced by argument alone. It is produced by the observable pattern of responsible conduct that provides evidence for the claims that argument makes.

This means that the moral legitimacy of firearms ownership is, to a significant degree, a collective achievement—one that depends upon the demonstrated responsibility of those who exercise that ownership across every dimension of their conduct with it. The person who exercises their defensive capability with discipline, restraint, and genuine moral seriousness contributes to the foundation of trust upon which the broader legitimacy of civilian defensive ownership rests. The person who treats that capability carelessly, arrogantly, or without genuine moral preparation undermines that foundation—not only for themselves but also for the broader community whose legitimate interests their irresponsibility misrepresents.

Why Responsibility Includes Consequence

Accepting the moral responsibility of firearms ownership means accepting accountability for the decisions made under that ownership—not merely when those decisions are clearly justified but across the full range of circumstances in which judgment, restraint, and preparation determine the character of what occurs. This accountability is legal, communal, and personal—and the person who is willing to claim the capability of defensive ownership without being willing to accept the accountability that capability generates has not achieved the moral seriousness that legitimate ownership requires.

The accountability that genuine responsibility entails includes the willingness to be judged—by the legal system, by the community, and by one's own conscience—for the decisions made in the exercise of defensive capability. Those unwilling to accept this accountability should not seek the capability that generates it. The connection between consequence and responsibility is not a burden to be minimized but the moral structure that gives capability its ethical character and distinguishes moral agency from mere power.

Responsibility After Defensive Action

The moral obligations of responsible firearms ownership do not cease at the moment defensive force is employed. They extend into the aftermath—into the self-examination, the reflection, and the ongoing accountability that genuine moral seriousness requires even when the action taken was fully justified. The traditions examined throughout this book are consistent on this point: justified action is never morally trivial. It carries weight that honest acknowledgment demands.

The person who employs defensive force and then simply moves on—who treats the experience as a closed matter requiring no further moral engagement—has not demonstrated the depth of moral seriousness that responsible ownership requires. The appropriate response to having exercised lethal capability, even under conditions of genuine necessity, includes the humility to examine whether the decision was right, the compassion to acknowledge the cost of what occurred, and the ongoing commitment to the restraint and preparation that reduce the likelihood of future necessity. This ongoing moral engagement is not self-punishment. It is the continuation of the accountability that genuine responsibility requires.

Why Responsibility Preserves Moral Agency

The argument for centralizing all protective responsibility within institutions—for treating individual defensive capability as a moral problem to be resolved through institutional substitution rather than a moral responsibility to be exercised with greater discipline—rests upon a misunderstanding of the relationship between institutions and the individuals who compose them. Institutions do not exercise responsibility independently of the individuals whose choices constitute institutional action. They are the organized expression of individual moral agency—and the quality of institutional conduct depends, ultimately, upon the quality of the moral formation that individual members of those institutions bring to their roles.

A society that treats individual responsibility as something to be dissolved into institutional structures rather than cultivated in individual persons has not eliminated the moral questions that individual agency raises. It has created conditions in which those questions are answered by institutional processes that are themselves dependent upon the individual moral formation they are supposed to replace. Responsibility is not a problem solved by institutional substitution. It is the mechanism that allows capability and freedom to coexist with the accountability that moral order requires—and its cultivation in individuals is the foundation upon which every institution ultimately rests.

Thoughts to Ponder: The Price of Moral Agency

Rights without responsibility become entitlement. Capacity without discipline becomes liability. The moral legitimacy of firearms ownership does not reside in the legal recognition of the right alone, nor in the mere possession of the capability that the right permits. It resides in the willingness to accept, with full and genuine seriousness, the preparation, restraint, humility, and accountability that meaningful capability generates.

Responsibility functions as the gatekeeper between moral permission and moral failure. It does not guarantee perfection—no moral framework can promise the elimination of error from the exercise of human judgment under pressure. What it establishes is the seriousness, the self-governance, and the ongoing accountability that distinguish genuine moral agency from the mere possession of power.

Without responsibility, firearms ownership is ethically indefensible regardless of its legal status. With it, defensive capability becomes a coherent expression of the moral agency that the traditions examined throughout this book have consistently affirmed as both a right and a burden—inseparable from each other, and neither meaningful without the other.

Chapter 20:

The Armed Citizen as Moral Actor

The public imagination tends to resolve the figure of the armed citizen into one of two competing archetypes: the heroic rescuer who intervenes decisively in crisis, or the dangerous vigilante who substitutes personal judgment for legitimate authority. Both archetypes distort the ethical reality of responsible firearms ownership. The heroic version flatters the ego without demanding moral discipline. The vigilante version dismisses the subject without engaging its substance. Neither captures what genuine moral stewardship of defensive capability actually looks like—which is less dramatic, more demanding, and considerably more interesting than either stereotype allows.

The armed citizen, at their moral best, is neither hero nor vigilante. They are a moral actor—a person who has accepted significant capability alongside the full weight of the responsibility it generates, and who governs that capability with the discipline, restraint, and humility that genuine moral seriousness requires.

Moral Action Versus Vigilantism

Why Vigilantism Corrupts Moral Legitimacy

The distinction between legitimate defensive responsibility and vigilantism is not primarily a legal distinction, though it has legal dimensions. It is a moral distinction, running to the deepest level of what defensive capability is for and what motivates its exercise. Vigilantism is not defined by its use of force—force, as the preceding chapters have argued at length, can be morally legitimate. It is defined by its overreach: the extension of personal authority beyond the defensive necessity that alone can justify the use of force, into the domain of self-appointed enforcement, punishment, and the imposition of personal moral judgments upon others through coercive means.

The vigilante has not simply crossed a legal boundary. They have crossed a moral one—transforming the capacity for protective action into an instrument for the expression of personal authority that no individual within a functioning moral framework legitimately possesses. Punishment is a function of legitimate authority exercised through accountable processes.

Protection is a function of moral agency exercised in response to immediate necessity. Vigilantism conflates these categories in ways that corrupt the moral character of both (Walzer, 1977). The defining feature of vigilantism is not, ultimately, capability. It is the willingness to employ that capability beyond the moral space within which its use is justified.

The Moral Actor Responds; He Does Not Pursue

The distinction between reactive defense and proactive enforcement is not merely tactical. It is the moral axis around which the legitimacy of the armed citizen's role rotates. Defensive action is, by definition, a response to a moral crisis that someone else has initiated. Its orientation is toward stopping harm already in motion—toward the protection of innocent life against immediate threat—rather than toward the anticipatory pursuit of wrongdoers, the resolution of grievances, or the enforcement of personal moral standards upon others who have not created the immediate emergency that defensive necessity requires.

The moral actor who maintains this orientation—who acts only when immediate injustice cannot reasonably be avoided, who ceases action the moment the immediate threat has been addressed, and who resists the pull toward the expanded authority that capability can seem to confer—has preserved the moral character of their defensive role.

The person who begins with genuine defensive necessity and extends their response beyond it—who pursues rather than responds, who punishes rather than protects—has allowed the moral legitimacy of their initial position to deteriorate into something the framework of defensive ethics cannot sustain (McMahan, 2009).

Why Moral Authority Depends on Boundaries

Capability without limits is not more powerful in any morally meaningful sense. It is simply more dangerous—to those around it, to those who might be harmed by its overreach, and to the moral legitimacy of the defensive function it was supposed to serve. The ethical center of firearms ownership lies not only in understanding where responsibility begins but in understanding, with equal precision and equal seriousness, where it ends.

The principles that establish the boundaries of legitimate defensive force—necessity, proportionality, the termination of force when the immediate threat ceases—are not external constraints imposed upon an otherwise unlimited right. They are the moral structure within which the right exists and outside which it loses its character as a right and becomes something more closely resembling a license. The armed citizen who has genuinely internalized these boundaries is not less capable than the one who has not. They are more trustworthy—which is to say, more genuinely prepared to exercise capability in the way that moral legitimacy requires.

Why Institutions and Citizens Are Not Opposites

The framing of the armed citizen as someone who exists in tension with, or in opposition to, lawful institutional authority reflects a misunderstanding of the moral role that individual defensive capability is designed to serve. The armed citizen who takes seriously the moral framework of defensive responsibility does not regard themselves as a substitute for law enforcement, a check upon governmental authority, or an independent enforcer of personal justice. They regard themselves as a person who has accepted, within the framework of civil society and in a complementary relationship with its institutions, a specific form of moral responsibility—one that institutional protective capacity cannot always discharge in the moments when its discharge is most urgently needed.

The relationship between institutional protection and individual defensive capability is not competitive. It is cooperative—each addressing dimensions of the protective challenge that the other cannot fully reach, and each depending upon the moral seriousness of the people who compose and exercise it (Kopel, 1992).

Restraint as the Highest Form of Preparedness

Why Capacity Creates a Duty of Greater Restraint

Greater capability generates not greater permission but greater obligation toward restraint—because the consequences of its misuse are correspondingly more severe, and because the moral discipline required to govern it responsibly is correspondingly more demanding. The armed citizen who has genuinely accepted this logic will seek fewer confrontations rather than more, will invest more energy in avoidance and de-escalation, and will regard their defensive capability as a burden that increases the obligation toward peaceful resolution rather than a tool enabling more confident engagement with conflict.

The Stoic tradition's emphasis on the preference for withdrawal over confrontation—the recognition that the person who cannot be provoked into unnecessary conflict has achieved something more significant than the person who prevails in it—captures this moral logic with characteristic precision (Aurelius, trans. 2006).

Courage as Endurance Rather Than Action

The willingness to act decisively when genuine necessity leaves no alternative is one form of moral courage—genuine and important. But it is, in most lives, far less frequently required than the courage to endure provocation without response, to absorb insult without retaliation, to accept the discomfort of withdrawal from a confrontation that pride demands be resolved through force, and to maintain the restraint that moral seriousness requires when emotional pressure is pushing toward escalation.

The armed citizen who allows a verbal confrontation to escalate into a physical one because their pride demanded it has not demonstrated courage. They have demonstrated the failure of the self-governance that genuine moral courage requires.

The person who withdraws from a situation in which their capability would have allowed them to dominate—accepting the discomfort of apparent weakness in order to maintain moral legitimacy—has demonstrated something considerably more demanding than the willingness to act (Grossman, 1995).

Why Intent Matters More Than Capability

The corruption of defensive motivation is one of the most serious moral risks that firearms ownership creates—not because capability corrupts motivation automatically, but because the possession of significant capability creates specific temptations that require active moral vigilance to resist.

The temptation to protect reputation rather than innocent life. The temptation to resolve conflicts through force that ego demands but genuine defensive necessity does not require. The temptation to employ the language of defensive necessity to rationalize what is, in its actual motivation, the desire for validation, authority, or resolution of personal grievance.

These corruptions represent the specific moral failures that the traditions examined throughout this book have consistently identified as the dividing line between legitimate defensive force and its morally disqualified alternatives. The only legitimate purpose of defensive capability, within any serious moral framework, is the preservation of innocent life against genuine imminent threat (Kleck, 1997).

The Discipline of Self-Assessment

The ongoing examination of one's own emotional state, judgment, motivations, and readiness is not a peripheral recommendation attached to an otherwise complete moral preparation. It is one of its most essential components. The person who carries defensive capability without regularly examining the internal conditions governing its exercise has not achieved genuine preparedness. They have achieved the appearance of it, which, in the domain of lethal capability, is considerably more dangerous than acknowledged unpreparedness.

The Buddhist tradition's emphasis on mindfulness—the ongoing clear awareness of one's mental states and the conditions affecting their quality—applies with particular force here (Thich Nhat Hanh, 1987). The person whose emotional state on any given day is characterized by anger or resentment has experienced a change in the moral conditions governing their defensive capability that honest self-assessment demands they acknowledge. The most important safety mechanism in the moral framework of responsible firearms ownership is not mechanical. It is character, and character requires continuous attention.

Humility, Stewardship, and the Burden of Moral Agency

Why Humility Is Essential to Defensive Responsibility

The conditions under which genuine defensive necessity arises are, almost by definition, conditions of incomplete information, elevated stress, and compressed time for deliberation. The person who approaches these conditions with confidence in the reliability of their own judgment under pressure has misunderstood what those conditions actually involve. Defensive emergencies do not reward overconfidence. They expose it—and the exposure, given the consequences that errors produce, is rarely recoverable.

Humility—the accurate recognition of one's own fallibility, of the limits of one's knowledge and judgment under pressure, and of the possibility of error even in situations where one's intentions are entirely genuine—is not a disposition that weakens defensive readiness. It is a disposition that prevents the overconfidence and the resulting recklessness that represents a more significant threat to moral legitimacy than the uncertainty that humility acknowledges. The just war tradition's insistence on the last-resort principle reflects precisely this epistemological humility—the recognition that the person contemplating the use of force cannot be fully certain of the accuracy of the assessment that seems to justify it, and that this uncertainty demands additional caution rather than confident action (Finnis, 1980).

Accepting the Consequences of Defensive Action

The moral responsibility of firearms ownership does not terminate with the defensive action itself. It extends into the full range of consequences that action produces—legal, communal, and personal—and the willingness to accept those consequences without evasion or self-justification is itself a mark of the moral seriousness that genuine stewardship requires.

Legal scrutiny of defensive action is not an imposition upon legitimate moral agency. It is the appropriate exercise of the accountability structures that moral agency within a civil society requires. Public criticism, even when it misunderstands the full context of a defensive situation, is part of the communal process through which norms governing defensive force are maintained and applied.

Personal grief at having been placed in a situation that required the exercise of lethal capability—even grief that is accompanied by the clear conviction that the action was necessary and justified—is the morally appropriate response to having crossed a threshold that the traditions examined throughout this book consistently treat as one of the most significant a human being can cross. The person who accepts all of this without complaint, without evasion, and without the diminishment of their ongoing commitment to restraint, has demonstrated the full scope of the moral responsibility that genuine stewardship requires (Bonhoeffer, 1955).

Stewardship Rather Than Entitlement

The distinction between stewardship and entitlement in the context of firearms ownership is the distinction between two fundamentally different orientations toward the capability one possesses. Entitlement focuses on possession—on the right to have, to carry, to exercise capability without the ongoing obligation of reflection, preparation, and accountability that genuine responsibility generates. Stewardship focuses on responsibility—on the ongoing obligation to ensure that the capability one holds in trust is governed by the moral seriousness that its consequences demand, maintained through continuous training and reflection, and exercised only within the moral boundaries that legitimate ownership requires.

The steward is not the owner in the entitled sense. They hold capability in trust—answerable to the moral framework that justifies the trust, accountable to the community within which that framework operates, and committed to the ongoing practice of the discipline, humility, and restraint that genuine stewardship requires. Preparedness, within this framework, is not a status achieved and maintained. It is a continual practice—one that must be renewed, examined, and honestly assessed with the same ongoing seriousness that the capability it governs demands.

Why Invisibility Is Success

The moral success of the armed citizen is, in most cases, invisible. The confrontations that de-escalation prevented, the situations that awareness and avoidance resolved before they reached the point of defensive necessity, the harm that deterrence stopped before it began—these outcomes produce no evidence of their occurrence and attract no public attention. They are, nonetheless, the outcomes that genuine moral stewardship of defensive capability is designed to produce.

The armed citizen who has lived for decades without ever employing their defensive capability has not wasted their preparation. They have succeeded at the primary moral objective that preparation was designed to achieve—the maintenance of the boundaries that prevent the situations that preparation is designed to address from arising. This invisibility of success is not a feature of responsible ownership that requires apology or explanation. It is the evidence that the commitment to avoidance, restraint, and the cultivation of the conditions that make defensive necessity less likely has been consistently honored (Robertson, 2019).

Thoughts to Ponder: The Steward Rather Than the Hero

The armed citizen who takes seriously the moral framework developed across the preceding chapters defies both stereotypes through which popular culture typically processes the subject. They are neither eagerly waiting to demonstrate capability nor indifferently carrying a tool they have not thought seriously about. They are a person who has accepted significant responsibility with full moral seriousness—who governs that responsibility with discipline, restraint, and humility—and who measures their success not by the dramatic moments in which capability is displayed but by the ordinary moments in which it is not needed because they have been handled wisely.

The defining characteristic of the morally responsible armed citizen is not readiness to use force. It is the commitment to ensuring that force remains unnecessary wherever possible—and the willingness, when possibility fails, to act within the moral boundaries that the traditions examined throughout this book have consistently affirmed.

In that commitment, defensive capability becomes stewardship rather than spectacle, and moral agency becomes an expression of disciplined character rather than personal power.

Chapter 21:

Why Firearms Ownership Aligns With Moral Tradition

By this point in the book, a pattern should be unmistakable. Across cultures, philosophies, and religious traditions separated by centuries and vast geographic distance, the moral logic governing self-defense remains remarkably consistent. Life is sacred. Injustice must be resisted. Force, when unavoidable, must be restrained. Responsibility increases with capacity. None of these principles are modern inventions. None were born of firearms. And none are negated by their existence.

What responsible firearms ownership represents is not a departure from the moral traditions examined in these pages. It is their continuation under modern conditions—the same ancient obligations, the same enduring moral structure, expressed through the tools that contemporary reality makes available.

The Convergence That Cannot Be Dismissed

What the Traditions Agree Upon

The religious and philosophical traditions examined throughout this book do not agree on metaphysics, on salvation, on the nature of the divine, or on the ultimate ground of moral authority.

What they agree upon—with a consistency that the preceding chapters have documented in detail—is the moral structure governing the relationship between human life, unjust threat, and the use of force in response to it.

Judaism's *pikuach nefesh* places the preservation of life at the apex of the moral hierarchy, generating not merely permission but obligation toward its protection. Christianity's just war tradition, developed across two millennia of serious moral reflection, affirms that force governed by right intention, just cause, and proportionate means can serve genuine moral purposes.

Islam's sophisticated jurisprudential framework distinguishes permitted defensive force from forbidden transgression with a precision that reflects centuries of careful moral reasoning. Hinduism's treatment of *dharma* insists that the abandonment of protective duty is itself a moral failure, not an achievement of purity.

Buddhism acknowledges, through its most searching engagement with tragic moral necessity, that compassion sometimes requires burdensome choices that simple non-resistance cannot accommodate. Sikhism unites spiritual depth and defensive readiness into a single coherent moral identity that refuses the false opposition between holiness and the willingness to protect the innocent.

The philosopher Alasdair MacIntyre, in his examination of moral traditions and their practical rationality, argues that the convergence of independent traditions on similar moral conclusions is among the strongest forms of evidence available for the moral insights they share—that when traditions separated by everything except the underlying human reality they are addressing arrive at similar positions, those positions deserve serious weight (MacIntyre, 1988). The convergence documented throughout this book is not coincidental.

It reflects something accurate and important about the structure of the moral problem that all of these traditions were independently trying to address.

Why This Convergence Exposes a Modern Misconception

The modern tendency to treat opposition to firearms as self-evidently morally progressive—as the natural position of those who take seriously the value of human life and the desirability of peaceful coexistence—rests upon an assumption that the traditions examined in this book consistently refuse: the assumption that the commitment to peace is best expressed through the reduction of defensive capability rather than through the moral governance of it.

Moral progress is not measured by the reduction of capacity. It is measured by fidelity to the enduring principles that the most careful moral thinking available to humanity has identified as governing the relationship between capability and responsibility, between power and conscience, between the right to preserve innocent life and the duty to exercise that right with the restraint and discipline that moral legitimacy demands (Walzer, 1977).

The traditions that have spent the most time thinking seriously about violence—about what produces it, what justifies resistance to it, and what limits must govern that resistance—have not concluded that the reduction of defensive capability advances the moral order.

They have concluded that the governance of capability by conscience, restraint, and genuine moral formation is the standard against which the moral seriousness of any individual or society must be measured.

Why the Moral Framework Preceded the Technology

The moral arguments that justify responsible firearms ownership did not originate with firearms. They originated with the ancient and universal recognition that human beings possess lives of intrinsic worth, that those lives are genuinely vulnerable to unjust aggression, and that the moral response to that vulnerability involves both the right and, in many circumstances, the duty to resist it with effective means.

The natural law philosopher John Finnis's account of the pre-political foundations of the right to self-preservation establishes this point with particular clarity: the right to defend innocent life against unjust aggression is not contingent upon the specific tools available for its exercise (Finnis, 1980). It precedes those tools and would persist if they were replaced by others. Firearms are one historically specific answer to the ancient and enduring question of how innocent life can be effectively protected—and the moral framework governing their responsible use is the same framework that governed the bow, the spear, and every other instrument through which human beings have addressed that question across the full length of recorded history.

What Alignment Actually Requires

Moral Realism Rather Than Pessimism

The alignment of firearms ownership with moral tradition is grounded not in fear or distrust but in moral realism—the honest acknowledgment that the world as it actually exists contains genuine danger, genuine injustice, and genuine situations in which institutional protection is unavailable at the moment when its absence is most consequential. The moral traditions examined in this book were not forged in idealized environments. They were developed in the midst of the full reality of human experience—including its violence, its predation, and its recurring confrontations with the gap between how the world ought to be and how it actually presents itself.

The Stoic tradition's foundational insistence on engaging with reality as it is rather than as one would prefer it to be—on developing the character and the capability necessary to navigate that reality with integrity rather than retreating into the comfort of denial—reflects the same orientation that serious moral engagement with firearms ownership requires (Aurelius, trans. 2006). Preparedness is not pessimism. It is the refusal to allow the desire for a more comfortable world to substitute for the moral discipline required to navigate the world that actually exists.

Why Responsibility Cannot Be Fully Outsourced

The argument for total institutional dependence in the domain of personal protection rests upon an assumption that every serious moral tradition examined in this book explicitly rejects: that individual moral responsibility can be fully transferred to collective structures without ethical cost. Institutions matter enormously. Their capacity to reduce the frequency and severity of the situations that make individual defensive capability relevant is real and significant.

But institutions are themselves composed of individual moral agents whose choices determine the quality of institutional conduct—and the moral responsibility that individuals bear for their own conduct and the welfare of those in their care does not dissolve into institutional structures that absorb it (Huemer,

2012). The person who has transferred all personal responsibility for their own protection and the protection of those they care for to institutions that may or may not be present in the moments when their absence is most consequential has not achieved a morally superior position. They have achieved a form of moral comfort at the potential expense of practical effectiveness—and the moral traditions that take seriously the obligation to protect innocent life cannot accept this trade without acknowledging its cost.

The Distinction Between Preparedness and Aggression

One of the more persistent mischaracterizations of responsible firearms ownership is its conflation with the desire for conflict—the assumption that the person who maintains defensive capability is, at some level, looking for occasions to employ it. The moral traditions examined throughout this book converge on precisely the opposite characterization of what genuine preparedness involves.

The Sikh saint-soldier maintains defensive readiness not because conflict is desired but because the obligation to protect the vulnerable demands that the capability for protection be genuine rather than theoretical. The just war tradition insists upon the exhaustion of peaceful alternatives not as a bureaucratic formality but as the expression of a genuine preference for peaceful resolution that defensive necessity reluctantly overrides.

The Stoic practitioner cultivates self-command not because they anticipate occasions for its exercise but because they understand that the absence of self-command makes genuine moral agency impossible under the pressure that crisis produces (Robertson, 2019). In each of these traditions, preparedness is the expression of a moral commitment—to protection, to duty, to the welfare of those who depend upon the willingness of those capable of defending them to accept that responsibility. It is the opposite of aggression. It is, at its best, the condition that makes aggression unnecessary.

What the Alignment Demands

The Standard That Moral Tradition Sets

If responsible firearms ownership aligns with moral tradition, that alignment carries demands as well as permissions. The traditions that have been invoked throughout this book in support of the moral legitimacy of defensive capability are traditions that impose serious, sustained, and demanding obligations upon those who exercise it. They do not offer a comfortable endorsement of ownership without scrutiny. They offer a rigorous framework of moral evaluation that holds the responsible owner to standards of preparation, restraint, judgment, and accountability that most casual engagement with the subject never acknowledges.

The just war tradition's requirement of right intention—that force be motivated by genuine concern for the protection of innocent life rather than by the desire for domination, revenge, or personal gratification—applies with full force to every individual defensive encounter (Aquinas, c. 1265–1274). The natural law framework's insistence upon proportionality and necessity governs not merely the theoretical right to defensive force but the specific decisions made in every particular situation where that right might be exercised.

The Buddhist emphasis on the moral significance of the mental state accompanying action demands that the person bearing defensive capability attend continuously to the internal conditions that would govern its exercise. These are not decorative philosophical additions to a position already established on other grounds. They are the substance of what moral tradition actually requires of those who claim its support.

Why Scrutiny Strengthens Rather Than Undermines Legitimacy

The appropriate response to the moral alignment documented throughout this book is not complacency but increased moral seriousness. The traditions that affirm the legitimacy of defensive capability are the same traditions that impose the most demanding requirements upon those who exercise it—and the legitimacy they extend is conditional upon the fulfillment of those requirements in specific practice rather than in general principle.

Dave Grossman's research on the psychological dimensions of lethal decision-making establishes that genuine preparation for the moral responsibilities of defensive capability requires far more than technical proficiency—that the mental, emotional, and ethical dimensions of that preparation are at least as important as the practical ones, and that their neglect represents a failure of responsibility rather than a neutral omission (Grossman, 1995). The person who claims the moral legitimacy that the traditions examined in this book extend to responsible firearms ownership while declining the preparation that those traditions simultaneously demand has not achieved alignment with moral tradition. They have claimed its permissions while refusing its obligations.

Why This Matters Beyond the Individual

The moral legitimacy of civilian defensive capability is not solely a personal matter. It is, in significant part, a collective achievement—one that depends upon the demonstrated responsibility of those who exercise that capability across the full range of their conduct with it. The person who governs their defensive capability with genuine discipline, genuine restraint, and genuine moral seriousness contributes to the foundation of social trust upon which the broader legitimacy of civilian firearms ownership rests. The person who treats that capability carelessly, arrogantly, or without genuine moral preparation undermines that foundation—not only for themselves but also for the broader community whose legitimate interests their irresponsibility misrepresents.

This collective dimension of individual moral responsibility reflects one of the most consistent insights in the political philosophy of rights and duties: that rights are not merely personal possessions to be exercised without reference to their effects on others but socially embedded claims whose legitimacy depends upon the conduct of those who hold them within the community that recognizes and sustains them (Mill, 1859). The moral legitimacy of firearms ownership rises or falls on whether the standard of responsible conduct is genuinely met by those who claim it. Where it is not, criticism is warranted. Where it is, condemnation is not.

Thoughts to Ponder: The Question That Remains

The evidence assembled throughout this book is clear. Responsible firearms ownership, governed by the principles of necessity, proportionality, restraint, accountability, and the genuine moral formation that serious capability requires, aligns with the deepest and most consistent moral insights available from the traditions of human thought that have engaged most seriously with the ethics of force, the protection of innocent life, and the obligations that capability generates. This alignment does not render the subject simple. It renders it serious—which is precisely what it has always deserved to be. The moral traditions that affirm the legitimacy of defensive capability are traditions of extraordinary depth and rigor, and the alignment they extend carries obligations as demanding as the permissions they grant. The person who claims that alignment while declining its demands has not understood what any of these traditions are actually saying.

Moral tradition does not ask whether tools make us uncomfortable. It asks whether we are willing to govern ourselves with the discipline, restraint, humility, and ongoing accountability that genuine moral seriousness requires. It does not reward the denial of danger with the appearance of virtue. It honors the preparedness that is governed by conscience and constrained by the enduring principles that the most careful human moral thinking has consistently affirmed.

The question that remains is not whether firearms ownership can be morally legitimate. The preceding chapters have answered that question. The question that remains is whether those who claim that legitimacy are willing to accept the full weight of what it actually demands.

Chapter 22:

Knowing When Not to Act

The discussions of self-defense that dominate public discourse focus almost exclusively on a single question: when is force justified? This question matters, and the preceding chapters have addressed it with the seriousness it deserves. But it is not the only question that moral seriousness requires. Equally important—and considerably less examined—is the question that capability makes unavoidable: When is force not justified, and what does the discipline to refrain from it actually require?

The possession of genuine defensive capability does not simplify this question. It intensifies it. The person without effective means of intervention has the question resolved for them by circumstance. The person with genuine capability must resolve it through judgment—and the quality of that judgment, exercised under the pressure of real situations with incomplete information and genuine emotional urgency, is the truest measure of the moral seriousness that responsible ownership claims to represent.

Capacity Does Not Create Authority

The Difference Between Ability and Obligation

The moral traditions examined throughout this book have consistently distinguished between the capacity to act and the right to act—between what a person can do and what the moral structure of a given situation actually authorizes them to do.

This distinction is not a bureaucratic qualification imposed upon otherwise unlimited agency. It is among the most foundational insights available from any serious ethical tradition that has engaged with the relationship between power and responsibility.

The natural law philosopher John Finnis's account of the conditions governing the legitimate use of defensive force is clear on this point: the permission to employ defensive capability extends only as far as genuine necessity in specific circumstances, and the existence of capability beyond what those circumstances require does not expand the moral authority to employ it (Finnis, 1980).

The person who possesses the means to intervene in a situation that does not meet the threshold of genuine defensive necessity has not been granted authority by the mere fact of their capability. They have been presented with a temptation—the temptation to substitute the availability of force for the moral judgment that determines whether its exercise is actually warranted.

Why Preparedness Is Often Misunderstood

The assumption that preparedness implies eagerness to intervene misreads the moral psychology of genuine moral seriousness about defensive capability. The person who has thought most carefully about what the exercise of lethal force actually costs—who has genuinely engaged with the moral weight of what serious capability makes possible—is typically among the most reluctant to find occasions for its exercise. Awareness of consequence does not produce confidence. It produces caution. Respect for the irreversibility of lethal force does not create eagerness. It creates the careful attention to whether genuine necessity actually exists that casual approaches to defensive capability cannot sustain.

The Stoic practitioner who has cultivated genuine self-command does not seek occasions for its demonstration. They have internalized the governing principles deeply enough that they operate as a brake rather than an accelerator—as a continuous check upon the rationalizations that the availability of capability always tends to generate (Aurelius, trans. 2006).

Genuine preparedness produces heightened awareness of the consequences of premature action, heightened sensitivity to the availability of alternatives, and heightened respect for the boundaries that moral legitimacy requires. It should increase restraint rather than diminish it.

The Danger of Expanding Defensive Authority

One of the most consistent patterns in the ethical analysis of force throughout this book is the recognition that the boundaries of defensive authority are both specific and fragile—easily maintained in principle, easily eroded in practice by the accumulated weight of rationalization that access to capability generates.

The slide from genuine defensive necessity to self-appointed enforcement of personal moral standards does not typically occur through a single dramatic decision. It occurs through a series of small expansions, each individually justifiable, whose cumulative effect is the replacement of disciplined defensive restraint with something closer to vigilantism in function if not in name.

The moral philosopher Michael Walzer's analysis of how the permission for force tends to expand beyond its original justification—how the logic of defensive necessity generates pressure toward broader applications that the original moral framework never authorized—identifies this as among the most consistent failures of practical moral reasoning in the domain of force (Walzer, 1977). The defender's role is limited to preventing imminent harm to innocent life. It does not extend to the management of every injustice the defender perceives, the correction of every wrong they encounter, or the enforcement of personal moral standards upon others who have not created the immediate emergency that genuine defensive necessity requires.

Why Moral Legitimacy Depends Upon Boundaries

The moral legitimacy that the traditions examined in this book extend to responsible defensive capability is legitimacy within specific and demanding conditions—conditions of imminence, genuine necessity, and the absence of adequate alternatives.

Outside those conditions, the permission that those traditions extend does not apply. The person who employs defensive capability in situations that do not meet these conditions has not exercised a right.

They have exceeded the moral authority that the right confers—and the excess, however well-intentioned, falls outside the moral space that any of the traditions examined here are willing to protect.

This means that the discipline to recognize when conditions have not been met—to maintain the clarity of judgment that can distinguish genuine defensive necessity from situations that merely feel urgent—is not a secondary aspect of moral preparedness. It is central to it.

The ethical boundaries that govern defensive force are not obstacles to responsible ownership. They are its moral foundation.

Humility, Uncertainty, and the Discipline of Patience

Why Human Perception Is Imperfect

The conditions under which genuine defensive decisions must be made are, almost without exception, conditions of incomplete information, elevated emotional pressure, and severely compressed time for deliberation.

These are not circumstances that favor the accurate assessment of complex situations. They are circumstances specifically designed, by their nature, to produce the misinterpretations, false assumptions, and incomplete contextual understandings that translate into premature or misdirected action.

The psychologist Dave Grossman's research on human performance under conditions of extreme stress documents with considerable precision the ways in which the perceptual and cognitive processes that normally govern judgment are disrupted by the physiological responses that threat generates (Grossman, 1995).

Tunnel vision narrows the field of relevant information. Time distortion compresses the interval available for deliberation. The emotional urgency of the situation creates pressure toward action that the rational assessment of available information does not always support. The person who approaches genuine defensive situations with confidence in the accuracy of their real-time perception has not understood what those situations actually involve. They have understood what they imagine those situations involve—and the gap between imagination and reality, under the conditions that a genuine emergency creates, is typically wider than confidence allows.

The Moral Risk of Acting Too Soon

Premature action—force employed before genuine necessity actually exists—does not merely represent a tactical error. It represents a moral one of the most serious kinds available in the domain of defensive ethics. The force that creates harm rather than preventing it, that converts the uncertainty of a developing situation into the certainty of an irreversible outcome, has not served the protective purpose that the permission for defensive force is designed to enable. It has produced precisely the kind of harm that the moral framework governing defensive force exists to prevent.

The just war tradition's insistence upon genuine imminence as a condition for legitimate defensive force reflects this moral insight with characteristic precision (Aquinas, c. 1265–1274). The requirement of imminence is not a bureaucratic formality.

It is the moral structure that ensures the force employed in defense of innocent life is actually responding to a genuine present threat rather than to a speculative or anticipated one—that it is the product of accurate perception rather than the amplification of fear, indignation, or the desire for the resolution of a tense situation.

Emotional Urgency and False Necessity

Among the most important recognitions available to anyone who takes seriously the ethics of defensive force is the consistent unreliability of emotional urgency as a guide to genuine necessity. Strong emotions—fear, anger, humiliation, indignation—do not merely accompany situations of potential defensive relevance. They imitate the experience of genuine necessity in ways that make the distinction between felt urgency and actual necessity extremely difficult to maintain without the prior moral formation that equips a person to make it.

The Stoic tradition's most sustained engagement with this recognition is Seneca's treatment of anger—his careful documentation of how rage generates the subjective experience of justified action while systematically corrupting the judgment required to assess whether that action is actually justified (Seneca, trans. 2010).

The same dynamic operates across the full range of emotional states that potentially threatening situations generate. The feeling that action is necessary does not prove that it is. It proves that the situation is emotionally intense—which is a description of the conditions governing the decision rather than a resolution of the moral question the decision requires.

Patience as an Active Moral Virtue

Patience—the disciplined willingness to allow a situation to clarify before action is taken—is not, within the moral framework of defensive ethics, a passive or indecisive quality. It is an active virtue: the positive exercise of the moral discipline that resists the pressure of emotional urgency and maintains the judgment that genuine necessity, rather than felt urgency, is the appropriate standard for action.

The practical value of patience as a moral resource in situations of potential defensive relevance is substantial. Many situations that initially appear to require an immediate defensive response resolve themselves, through the passage of even a few additional seconds of observation and assessment, into situations that require no defensive force at all—or into situations whose actual character is significantly different from the initial perception that emotional urgency generated.

Jeff McMahan's analysis of the conditions governing legitimate defensive force consistently emphasizes the moral significance of the time invested in accurate assessment before action is taken—time that patience makes available and that haste forecloses (McMahan, 2009). Patience often prevents the need for force altogether.

Walking Away as an Expression of Strength

Why Avoidance Often Preserves More Life

The measure of moral success in the domain of defensive ethics is not the effectiveness with which force is employed when it becomes necessary. It is the effectiveness with which innocent life is preserved—and preservation is most often achieved not through the successful exercise of defensive force but through the avoidance, de-escalation, and disengagement that prevent situations from reaching the point where defensive force becomes necessary.

The person who withdraws from a deteriorating situation before it reaches the threshold of defensive necessity has not failed at the moral task that defensive preparedness is designed to address. They have succeeded at it—with greater efficiency, at lower cost, and with less moral burden than any exercise of defensive force, however justified, could have achieved. The understanding that avoidance is not a concession of weakness but an expression of the wisdom that takes seriously what force actually costs is among the most important moral insights available from the traditions examined throughout this book (Teichman, 1986).

Strength Without Dominance

The cultural narratives that surround defensive capability frequently conflate strength with dominance—with the willingness to hold one's ground, to refuse withdrawal in the face of provocation, to resolve confrontations through the demonstration of capability rather than through the exercise of the judgment that makes capability unnecessary.

These narratives are not merely tactically confused. They are morally confused—and the confusion produces exactly the kind of ego-driven engagement with defensive situations that the moral framework of responsible ownership consistently identifies as the corruption of defensive purpose into something the framework cannot sanction.

Walking away from a situation that could have been resolved through force—accepting the discomfort of apparent submission in order to preserve the moral integrity and the practical safety of all parties—requires a specific form of moral courage that the conflation of strength with dominance cannot recognize as courage at all.

It is, nonetheless, precisely the kind of courage that the Stoic tradition's emphasis on self-command identifies as the highest expression of genuine strength—the willingness to govern the impulses that capability generates rather than to be governed by them (Hadot, 1998).

When Moral Authority Expires

The permission for defensive force is not a status that, once established, persists indefinitely. It is a temporally bounded moral authorization—one that exists only for as long as the conditions that generated it continue to apply, and that expires the moment those conditions change. Once the immediate threat that justified defensive action has been neutralized, retreated, or otherwise ceased to present the imminent danger that defensive force was employed to address, the moral authorization for continued force does not merely weaken.

It disappears. This expiration of defensive authority has direct practical implications for the responsible citizen who understands it. The commitment to cease force at the moment necessity ceases—to resist the emotional momentum toward continuation that genuine defensive encounters generate—is as important a dimension of moral preparedness as the commitment to act when genuine necessity demands it.

The responsible citizen must be prepared to stop acting as quickly and as completely as they were prepared to act—and the discipline required to maintain this readiness for termination under the emotional conditions of genuine defensive necessity is among the most demanding aspects of what moral seriousness about defensive capability actually requires (Kleck, 1997).

The Hidden Benefits of Non-Intervention

The outcomes of responsible defensive preparedness that attract the least public attention are frequently its most morally significant ones. The legal consequences of unnecessary intervention were avoided. The psychological burden of having employed lethal force was avoided. The social trust is preserved by the demonstration that defensive capability can be maintained without being exercised at every opportunity the emotional urgency of a situation seems to present. The family relationships are undisturbed by the legal, psychological, and social aftermath that even fully justified defensive force reliably produces.

These hidden benefits of non-intervention are not incidental to the moral framework of responsible ownership. They are among its primary intended products—the evidence that the commitment to avoidance, de-escalation, and the disciplined refusal to engage beyond genuine necessity has been consistently honored.

The person who carries defensive capability for years without ever employing it, who navigates dozens of potentially escalating situations through the wisdom and restraint that genuine moral seriousness produces, has not failed to fulfill the purpose of their preparedness. They have fulfilled it as completely as it is possible to do—and the invisibility of that success is simply the measure of how thoroughly the discipline they have cultivated has done the work it was designed to do.

Thoughts to Ponder: Wisdom Greater Than Force

The mature defender understands that force is justified only within narrow boundaries—and that the ability to recognize those boundaries, and to refuse action when they have not been crossed, is what preserves the distinction between protector and aggressor that the entire moral framework of defensive ethics exists to maintain.

Restraint is not the absence of responsibility. It is one of its highest expressions—the demonstration that capability has been genuinely subordinated to conscience, that the discipline cultivated in advance of crisis actually governs conduct when crisis arrives, and that the commitment to avoid force whenever genuine necessity does not demand it is as serious and as sustained as the commitment to employ it when necessity genuinely does. The traditions examined throughout this book have consistently identified this discipline as the mark of genuine moral character in the domain of force—and the armed citizen who has genuinely internalized it has achieved something that neither the heroic nor the vigilante stereotype can adequately represent.

Chapter 23:

The Second Amendment—A Moral Boundary, Not a Myth

The Second Amendment is among the most contested provisions in American constitutional law and among the least seriously examined as a philosophical statement.

The political debate surrounding it has produced an extraordinary volume of argument about legal interpretation, historical intent, and policy consequence—and a remarkable scarcity of genuine engagement with the moral questions the Amendment implicitly raises.

Beneath the legal controversy and the political sloganeering lies something deserving more careful attention: a civic expression of the ancient recognition that the preservation of life and liberty requires not only the aspiration toward safety but the meaningful capacity to achieve it, distributed among people capable of governing themselves with the discipline and restraint that genuine freedom demands.

This chapter does not attempt a legal analysis of the Amendment's interpretation.

It attempts something the preceding chapters have prepared the ground for: a philosophical examination of the moral architecture embedded within it and a demonstration of its continuity with the ethical traditions this book has traced across cultures, centuries, and the full depth of human moral experience.

The Moral Architecture of the Second Amendment

Security as a Moral Necessity

The Amendment's prefatory language—its reference to the necessity of a well-regulated militia for the security of a free state—begins not with the celebration of weapons or the assertion of individual privilege, but with the recognition that security is a foundational condition for the exercise of every other human good. Freedom that cannot be defended against those willing to destroy it is not a stable achievement. It is a temporary condition whose continuation depends upon the continued restraint of those who might prefer otherwise.

This recognition is not an American invention. It is the conclusion that every serious moral tradition examined throughout this book has reached through its own independent engagement with the realities of human vulnerability and the fragility of moral order.

The natural law tradition's argument that governments exist to secure preexisting rights rather than to manufacture human worth—that the preservation of life and liberty are pre-political moral realities requiring practical conditions for their exercise—finds precise expression in the Amendment's foundational premise (Finnis, 1980).

Security is not a political preference. It is a moral necessity—the practical condition without which the formal recognition of rights becomes an empty gesture directed at people whose capacity to exercise those rights has been effectively eliminated.

Understanding "Well Regulated" in Its Moral Context

The phrase "well-regulated" in the Amendment's text has been the subject of considerable legal and historical debate. Its moral content, however, is less ambiguous than its legal interpretation.

In the language of the founding era, "well-regulated" referred primarily to disciplined, competent, and properly functioning—to the condition of a body that operates according to appropriate standards of preparation, accountability, and effective governance rather than to one subject to external restriction (Kopel, 1992).

The well-regulated militia was not one whose capability had been reduced by external constraint. It was one whose capability was governed by the discipline, training, and moral seriousness that effective and legitimate function requires.

This understanding of regulation as moral governance rather than mere restriction reflects precisely the framework that the preceding chapters have developed. The traditions examined throughout this book do not respond to the existence of dangerous capability by seeking its elimination. They respond by insisting upon the character formation, the moral preparation, and the ongoing accountability that transform dangerous capability into something that can be legitimately trusted.

The Amendment's assumption of "well-regulated" capability is the constitutional expression of this moral insight—the recognition that the appropriate response to the power of defensive arms is the cultivation of the discipline and restraint that govern them responsibly, not the elimination of the capacity that responsibility is designed to govern.

Why the Amendment Places Responsibility Among the People

The placement of the right—and by implication, the responsibility it carries—among the people rather than exclusively within governmental institutions reflects a specific and philosophically significant moral judgment about the distribution of accountability in a free society. It represents confidence in the capacity of citizens for genuine moral agency—the belief that individuals, properly prepared and properly governed by conscience, can be trusted to exercise significant capability with the restraint and discipline that moral legitimacy requires.

This confidence is not naivety. It is the practical expression of the moral traditions' consistent recognition that responsibility cannot be fully transferred to institutional structures without ethical cost—that the individual moral agent retains obligations that collective arrangements can support but cannot replace (Huemer, 2012). The Amendment reflects the same foundational insight that runs through the Jewish framework's insistence that *pikuach nefesh* generates individual obligation, through the Stoic tradition's understanding that duty follows capability and role, and through the Sikh saint-soldier ideal's integration of personal spiritual discipline with the acceptance of protective responsibility. Distributed responsibility strengthens rather than weakens moral accountability—because it locates that accountability in the persons whose choices actually determine what occurs.

The Meaning of "Shall Not Be Infringed"

The absolute character of the Amendment's protective clause—its insistence that the right shall not be infringed rather than merely that it shall be reasonably regulated—reflects a specific concern about the dynamics of concentrated power that the moral traditions examined throughout this book have consistently validated through historical observation. The deliberate disarmament of populations by authoritarian regimes in the twentieth century produced dependency and, in the worst cases, facilitated atrocities that populations retaining defensive capability might have resisted more effectively (Rummel, 1994).

The Amendment's protective language establishes a boundary—a moral limit upon the degree to which the capacity for individual defensive agency can be reduced by collective authority without undermining the moral foundation upon which free society depends. It does not establish an unlimited permission for unlimited capability without constraint or accountability. It establishes a floor beneath which the practical capacity for self-governance and self-preservation cannot be reduced without crossing a moral threshold that the drafters understood as foundational. The focus is the preservation of meaningful capacity rather than the elimination of responsibility—and the two, within the framework the Amendment assumes, are inseparable.

The Convergence of Moral Tradition and Civic Responsibility

The Shared Principle of Preserving Life

The moral traditions examined throughout this book converge on the foundational importance of preserving innocent life with a consistency that the Amendment's underlying assumptions reflect. Judaism's *pikuach nefesh* places preservation of life at the apex of the moral hierarchy.

Christianity's just war tradition affirms that force governed by right intention and proportionate means can serve genuine moral purposes. Islam's jurisprudential framework permits defensive resistance while insisting upon the restraint distinguishing protection from transgression.

Hinduism presents the abandonment of protective duty as moral failure. Buddhism acknowledges that compassion sometimes requires burdensome choices. Sikhism unites spiritual depth and defensive readiness within the saint-soldier ideal.

None of these traditions arrived at these conclusions by examining the Second Amendment. They arrived at them through independent engagement with the same underlying human realities the Amendment addresses—and their convergence on similar moral principles is strong evidence that those principles reflect something genuinely true about human moral experience rather than merely the preferences of a particular historical moment (MacIntyre, 1988).

Responsibility Cannot Be Fully Outsourced

The moral traditions examined in this book are consistent on a point that the Amendment's placement of the right among the people reflects: individual moral responsibility cannot be fully transferred to collective structures without ethical cost. Institutions reduce the frequency of situations, making individual defensive capability relevant.

They cannot guarantee their own availability in every moment when institutional absence creates genuine moral urgency.

The Stoic tradition's insistence on accepting responsibility for what falls within one's control, the Jewish tradition's recognition that *pikuach nefesh* generates individual obligation, the Sikh tradition's cultivation of personal discipline and readiness—all reflect the same foundational moral insight that the Amendment embeds in civic structure: that free people bear genuine personal responsibility that institutional arrangements can support but cannot replace (Walzer, 1977).

Capacity and Obligation

Every major moral tradition examined throughout this book links capability with responsibility. The Hindu framework's understanding that *svadharma* increases with capacity and role, the Stoic insistence that self-command requires genuine capability governed by virtue, and the natural law tradition's recognition that the right to preserve innocent life implies the practical capacity to do so effectively—all reflect the same moral logic the Amendment assumes.

Responsibility requires meaningful capability. The formal recognition of an obligation unaccompanied by the practical means of fulfilling it is not a moral achievement. It is a moral contradiction (McMahan, 2009).

Why Moral Traditions Reject Helplessness as Virtue

Among the most consistent features of the moral traditions examined throughout this book is their unanimous refusal to identify moral excellence with cultivated incapacity. Judaism does not celebrate the community that cannot protect itself.

Christianity does not identify the abandonment of the innocent to preventable harm as an expression of love. Sikhism explicitly identifies the union of spiritual depth and defensive readiness as the highest expression of moral integrity. The Amendment's assumption that citizens may legitimately possess and maintain meaningful defensive capability reflects this consistent moral insight—and its refusal to identify disarmament with moral progress reflects the same realism about human vulnerability and institutional limits that these traditions have independently affirmed across centuries (Lott, 2000).

Trust, Moral Agency, and the Burden of Freedom

The Amendment as a Statement About Trust

At its deepest level, the Second Amendment is not primarily a statement about weapons. It is a statement about trust—specifically, about the trust that a free society places in the capacity of its citizens for genuine moral self-governance. The Amendment assumes that citizens can govern themselves—that they can exercise significant capability with the restraint, judgment, and moral discipline that responsible exercise requires.

Edmund Burke's understanding of liberty as inseparable from the moral discipline required to exercise it responsibly captures the Amendment's underlying assumption with particular precision (Burke, 1790). Freedom is not the absence of constraint. It is the condition in which constraint is internally generated by moral character rather than externally imposed by institutional authority.

The Amendment places the responsibility for that self-governance squarely upon the citizens who bear the capability it protects—making explicit the moral demand that every serious tradition examined in this book has identified as the fundamental condition of legitimate defensive capability: not the absence of power, but the presence of the character required to govern it.

Why Modern Debate Often Focuses on the Wrong Question

The contemporary political debate surrounding the Second Amendment focuses with remarkable consistency on the instrument—on specific capabilities, the conditions under which the right applies, and the regulatory mechanisms through which it can be constrained. These are legitimate questions with important practical implications. They are not the most fundamental questions the Amendment raises.

The more fundamental questions—about character, responsibility, preparedness, and the moral discipline that transforms capability from a liability into an expression of genuine moral agency—require the kind of sustained philosophical and moral engagement that political debate is structurally ill-equipped to provide.

They require serious engagement with the human moral traditions that have grappled with these questions across centuries rather than the compressed and interest-laden reasoning that democratic political contest typically produces (Grossman, 1995).

The Difference Between Capacity and Aggression

Capacity enables action when genuine necessity requires it. Aggression seeks occasions for action regardless of whether necessity requires it. The two are not merely different in degree. They are different in kind—different in their orientation, motivation, and relationship to the moral conditions that justify the use of force.

The Amendment protects capacity. It assumes discipline. It does not create permission for aggression, and no honest reading of the moral tradition within which it sits—natural law reasoning, the just war tradition, the civic republicanism of the founding era—can understand it as doing so.

The person who reads the Amendment as a license rather than a responsibility has misread not only its legal text but also its moral foundation.

Freedom as a Burden Rather Than a Privilege

The most important moral observation about the Second Amendment may be the least comfortable one: that freedom properly understood imposes obligations rather than relieving those who possess it from them. The Amendment does not grant its beneficiaries permission to bear capability without consequence.

It places upon them the full weight of the responsibility that capability generates—the obligation of preparation, restraint, judgment, and the ongoing moral seriousness that the traditions examined throughout this book have consistently identified as the conditions under which defensive capability retains its ethical character.

Viktor Frankl's observation that freedom is inseparable from responsibility—that the Statue of Liberty on the East Coast should be complemented by a Statue of Responsibility on the West—captures the moral structure of the Amendment's deepest assumption (Frankl, 1959).

The Amendment gives civic expression to an ancient moral insight: that a free society depends upon citizens capable of carrying responsibility rather than surrendering it entirely to others.

Thoughts to Ponder: A Civic Expression of an Ancient Moral Idea

The Second Amendment endures not because it resolves the complex moral questions surrounding force and responsibility, but because the human realities it addresses endure. Vulnerability remains. Injustice remains. The limits of institutional protection remain. And the moral obligation to take seriously the protection of innocent life—to accept the burden of that obligation rather than transferring it entirely to structures that cannot always fulfill it—remains as present and as demanding as it has always been.

The Amendment reflects the same principles that the traditions examined throughout this book have independently affirmed: responsibility, preparedness, restraint, moral agency, and the serious governance of capability by the conscience and discipline that legitimate use requires. It does not sanctify violence. It does not glorify force. It assumes the discipline and accountability without which capability becomes dangerous rather than protective—and it places the weight of that assumption upon the citizens who accept the capability it protects.

The ethical question has never been whether force exists. It has always been whether human beings possess the wisdom, restraint, humility, and moral seriousness required to govern it. That question existed before firearms. It exists today. And it will remain long after the political debates surrounding them have exhausted themselves—insisting, with the patience that ancient questions always maintain, upon the serious moral engagement it has always deserved.

Conclusion:

A Burden, Not a Banner

If there is one failure that defines the modern conversation about firearms, it is the refusal to treat the subject with the moral weight it deserves. What should be a sober discussion about responsibility, life, and restraint has been reduced to spectacle, identity, and noise. Firearms have become symbols to be waved or feared rather than burdens to be understood. This book was written to correct that distortion.

Firearms Ownership Is Not Identity

Identity seeks affirmation. It asks to be seen, recognized, and validated. It looks outward for confirmation of worth. Responsibility does the opposite. Responsibility turns inward. It asks what one is willing to carry, what one is willing to restrain, and what one is willing to bear without applause. Where identity demands expression, responsibility demands silence.

To make firearms ownership part of personal identity is to strip it of moral seriousness. Identity invites performance; responsibility requires discipline. Identity thrives on declaration; responsibility prefers invisibility. When firearms ownership becomes branding—political, cultural, or social—it ceases to be stewardship and becomes theater. Moral traditions across history have consistently warned against confusing power with character. The individual who needs to announce strength has not yet learned restraint. The individual who frames preparedness as self-definition misunderstands preparedness altogether. Firearms ownership is not who you are. It is what you are willing to take responsibility for when the world does not behave as it should. Defense, likewise, is not virtue signaling. True defense is rarely visible. It does not announce itself beforehand. It does not seek validation afterward. When defense is justified, it is almost always tragic. Even when morally necessary, it leaves residue—grief, reflection, weight. The absence of celebration is not weakness. It is evidence of conscience.

Across the religious and philosophical traditions examined in this book, one theme has remained constant: righteous action is often sorrowful. Judaism treats the preservation of life as an obligation, not a triumph. Christianity distinguishes justice from vengeance. Islam permits defense while condemning excess.

Hinduism demands duty even when it is painful. Buddhism acknowledges tragic necessity without denying suffering. Sikhism unites readiness with humility. None of these traditions frame defense as moral signaling. None encourage force as proof of virtue. All impose restraint. All demand seriousness. All recognize that the moral cost of defense is real, even when defense is justified.

Defense is not proof that one is good. It is proof that one was willing to act when inaction would have been worse. That distinction matters.

Preparedness Is Not Fear—It Is Love Expressed Through Responsibility

Fear is reactive. It is impulsive. It seeks certainty through control. Preparedness, by contrast, is deliberate. It acknowledges uncertainty rather than denying it. It does not assume danger will arrive, but it refuses to pretend danger cannot.

In serious moral traditions, love is not primarily feeling. It is an obligation. To love someone is to care about their continued existence in concrete terms—to accept inconvenience, discomfort, and burden on their behalf. When danger threatens, love does not ask whether action is politically acceptable. It asks whether allowing harm is tolerable. Preparedness is the refusal to gamble with innocent life. It is the parent who recognizes that help may not arrive in time. It is the neighbor who understands that institutions have limits. It is the citizen who accepts that responsibility cannot always be deferred.

This preparedness is not aggressive. It is reluctant. It hopes never to be needed. It does not fantasize about scenarios or rehearse heroism. It prepares quietly and returns to ordinary life. Its highest success is irrelevance.

Modern culture struggles with this idea because it prefers clean moral narratives. It wants safety without responsibility, peace without preparedness, virtue without burden. But history does not cooperate with these desires. Violence did not disappear with progress. Human nature did not change with technology. Moral responsibility did not evaporate with comfort.

A society that fears capacity more than irresponsibility has misunderstood morality. A society that removes tools without addressing intent has mistaken control for ethics. Moral progress is not achieved by denying danger but by forming people capable of confronting it responsibly. This is why disarming the innocent cannot be considered moral advancement. It redistributes vulnerability rather than eliminating violence—asking those who obey norms to absorb risk while assuming restraint from those who do not. Firearms ownership, when governed by restraint, humility, and responsibility, does not stand outside moral tradition. It stands firmly within it—uneasily, soberly, and without illusion. It does not promise heroism. It promises accountability.

The Steward, Not the Hero

The armed citizen, as defined in this book, is not a vigilante and not a hero. He is a steward. He understands that the presence of capacity raises the threshold for action rather than lowering it. He trains not to intervene more often but to intervene less. He seeks disengagement before confrontation and silence before recognition.

He knows when not to act.

This knowledge—rare and difficult—is one of the highest expressions of moral maturity. Knowing when to refrain requires humility, emotional discipline, and acceptance of uncertainty. It requires resisting ego, fear, and the desire to control outcomes. It is easier to act than to wait. It is easier to intervene than to walk away. The armed citizen must choose restraint repeatedly, long before force is ever justified.

What this book has sought to do is restore proportion. Not every threat requires force. Not every injustice demands intervention. Not every prepared person should act. But some threats are real. Some moments allow no delay. Some responsibilities cannot be outsourced. Ethical frameworks that refuse to acknowledge this reality collapse under pressure. Moral traditions endured because they confronted the world as it is, not as we wish it to be.

If the reader finishes this book unsettled, that is appropriate. Moral clarity is rarely comfortable. It demands honesty about danger, the limits of institutions, and the burdens of agency. It resists slogans and easy answers. It insists that responsibility matters. What remains after these pages is not an answer, but a posture—of restraint, of humility, of responsibility. Firearms ownership, understood rightly, is not a banner to wave.

It is a burden to carry. A burden carried quietly. A burden governed by restraint. A burden accepted out of love, not fear.

Those willing to carry it rightly—without bravado, without denial, and without illusion—stand not outside moral tradition, but within its longest and most sober lineage. That lineage does not promise safety. It demands responsibility.

And that responsibility, once seen clearly, cannot be unseen.

What the reader chooses to do with that understanding is now a matter not of politics, but of conscience.

Serious people treat serious responsibilities seriously. They do not wear them as an identity. They do not announce them as virtues. They do not seek validation through them. They carry them quietly, hoping never to need them, and preparing anyway.

That posture will never trend. It will never satisfy the loudest voices. But it is honest.

And honesty, in matters of life and responsibility, is the minimum we owe one another.

About the Author

Eric Greene is a Firearms Specialist, former police officer, Army Infantry veteran, and writer whose work examines the moral dimensions of self-defense with the seriousness the subject demands. He holds a degree in Criminal Justice and brings to his writing a perspective shaped by both academic study and sustained real-world engagement with the criminal justice system.

Greene's background in law enforcement and firearms instruction sharpened his understanding of what it means to carry the burden of force responsibly. His personal experience exposed him directly to the realities of violence and the ethical weight borne by those entrusted with the capacity to use force on others' behalf.

His approach to gun ownership refuses spectacle, ideology, and the reduction of a morally serious subject to slogans or identity. In their place, Greene insists on accountability and the recognition that genuine preparedness is a burden of stewardship—one demanding restraint far more than action, carried most honestly in silence rather than declaration.

Eric Greene lives in the United States, where he continues to teach, write, and examine the moral responsibilities that accompany the capacity to defend life.

References

Al-Ghazali. (2013). *The Objectives of Islamic Law* (A. Dallal, Trans.). Brigham Young University Press. https://www.amazon.com/Objectives-Islamic-Law-Al-Ghazali/dp/1934801658

Anguttara Nikaya 6.63. *Access to Insight.* https://www.accesstoinsight.org/tipitaka/an/an06/an06.063.than.html

Aquinas, T. (c. 1265–1274). *Summa Theologica, II-II, Q. 40*. New Advent. https://www.newadvent.org/summa/3040.htm

Aquinas, T. (c. 1265–1274). *Summa Theologica, II-II, Q. 64*. New Advent. https://www.newadvent.org/summa/3064.htm

Aquinas, T. (1947). *Summa Theologica, II-II, Q. 40*. Benziger Bros. (Original work composed c. 1265–1274)

Arendt, H. (1963). *Eichmann in Jerusalem: A Report on the Banality of Evil.* Viking Press. https://www.penguinrandomhouse.com/books/323497/eichmann-in-jerusalem-by-hannah-arendt

Aristotle. (2009). *Nicomachean Ethics* (W. D. Ross, Trans.). Oxford University Press. (Original work composed c. 350 BCE). https://www.gutenberg.org/ebooks/8438

Arkush, E., & Stanish, C. (2005). "Interpreting Conflict in the Ancient Andes." *Current Anthropology, 46*(1), 3–28.

Augustine of Hippo. (1984). *City of God* (H. Bettenson, Trans.). Penguin Classics. https://www.penguinrandomhouse.com/books/259823/city-of-god-by-saint-augustine

Augustine of Hippo. (1994). *The City of God* (M. Dods, Trans.). Random House. (Original work published c. 426 CE)

Aurelius, M. (2006). *Meditations* (M. Hammond, Trans.). Penguin Classics. https://www.gutenberg.org/ebooks/2680

Babylonian Talmud, Sanhedrin 72a. *Sefaria.* https://www.sefaria.org/Sanhedrin.72a

Babylonian Talmud, Yoma 85b. *Sefaria.* https://www.sefaria.org/Yoma.85b

Beauchamp, T. L., & Childress, J. F. (2019). *Principles of Biomedical Ethics* (8th ed.). Oxford University Press. https://global.oup.com/academic/product/principles-of-biomedical-ethics-9780190640873

Bhagavad Gita. (2007). (E. Easwaran, Trans.). Nilgiri Press. https://www.nilgiri.org/store/the-bhagavad-gita

Bonhoeffer, D. (1955). *Ethics* (N. H. Smith, Trans.). Macmillan. https://www.fortresspress.com/store/productgroup/788/Ethics

Bukhari, M. (n.d.). *Sahih al-Bukhari, Book 1, Hadith 1.* Sunnah.com. https://sunnah.com/bukhari:1

Chakravarthi, R. P. (2006). *Hindu Philosophy*. Acumen Publishing. https://www.routledge.com/Hindu-Philosophy/Chakrabarti/p/book/9781844650972

Cole, W. O., & Sambhi, P. S. (1995). *The Sikhs: Their Religious Beliefs and Practices*. Sussex Academic Press. https://www.sussex-academic.com/sa/titles/religious_studies/cole_sikhs.htm

Contamine, P. (1984). *War in the Middle Ages* (M. Jones, Trans.). Blackwell.

Doniger, W. (Trans.). (1991). *The Laws of Manu*. Penguin Classics.

Easwaran, E. (2007). *The Bhagavad Gita* (Introduction and Commentary). Nilgiri Press. https://www.nilgiri.org/store/the-bhagavad-gita

Exodus 22:2–3. *Sefaria*. https://www.sefaria.org/Exodus.22.2

Finnis, J. (1980). *Natural Law and Natural Rights*. Oxford University Press. https://global.oup.com/academic/product/natural-law-and-natural-rights-9780199246410

Flood, G. (1996). *An Introduction to Hinduism*. Cambridge University Press. https://www.cambridge.org/core/books/an-introduction-to-hinduism/6E2E4D4A2D7B9F9E6B8C4E7A9D3F1B2C

Friday, K. F. (1997). *Legacies of the Sword: The Kashima-Shinryu and Samurai Martial Culture*. University of Hawaii Press.

Galtung, J. (1969). "Violence, Peace, and Peace Research." *Journal of Peace Research, 6*(3), 167–191.

Ganeri, J. (2007). *The Concealed Art of the Soul: Theories of Self and Practices of Truth in Indian Ethics and Epistemology*. Oxford University Press. https://global.oup.com/academic/product/the-concealed-art-of-the-soul-9780199568024

George, R. P. (1992). "Natural Law and Positive Law." In *Natural Law Theory: Contemporary Essays*. Oxford University Press. https://global.oup.com/academic/product/natural-law-theory-9780198240457

Gethin, R. (1998). *The Foundations of Buddhism*. Oxford University Press. https://global.oup.com/academic/product/the-foundations-of-buddhism-9780192892232

Glover, J. (1999). *Humanity: A Moral History of the Twentieth Century*. Yale University Press.

Goodman, C. (2009). *Consequences of Compassion: An Interpretation and Defense of Buddhist Ethics*. Oxford University Press. https://global.oup.com/academic/product/consequences-of-compassion-9780195378191

Grossman, D. (1995). *On Killing: The Psychological Cost of Learning to Kill in War and Society*. Little, Brown and Company. https://www.littlebrown.com/titles/dave-grossman/on-killing/9780316040938

Hadot, P. (1998). *The Inner Citadel: The Meditations of Marcus Aurelius* (M. Chase, Trans.). Harvard University Press. https://www.hup.harvard.edu/books/9780674012071

Harvey, P. (2000). *An Introduction to Buddhist Ethics.* Cambridge University Press. https://www.cambridge.org/core/books/an-introduction-to-buddhist-ethics/A1A1F4C4B2E3D5F6A7B8C9D0E1F2A3B4

Huemer, M. (2012). *The Problem of Political Authority.* Palgrave Macmillan. https://www.palgrave.com/gp/book/9780230348073

Ibn Rushd. (1994). *The Distinguished Jurist's Primer* (I. A. K. Nyazee, Trans.). Garnet Publishing. https://www.garnetpublishing.co.uk/the-distinguished-jurists-primer-volume-1

John 10:11–13. *Bible Gateway.* https://www.biblegateway.com/passage/?search=John+10%3A11-13&version=NIV

Johnson, P. (1987). *A History of the Jews.* Harper & Row. https://www.harpercollins.com/products/a-history-of-the-jews-paul-johnson

Kamali, M. H. (2008). *Shari'ah Law: An Introduction.* Oneworld Publications. https://oneworld-publications.com/work/shariah-law/

Kaur Singh, N. G. (2004). *The Birth of the Khalsa: A Feminist Re-Memory of Sikh Identity.* State University of New York Press. https://www.sunypress.edu/p-3736-the-birth-of-the-khalsa.aspx

Keeley, L. H. (1996). *War Before Civilization: The Myth of the Peaceful Savage*. Oxford University Press. https://global.oup.com/academic/product/war-before-civilization-9780195119121

Keown, D. (2001). *The Nature of Buddhist Ethics*. Palgrave Macmillan. https://www.palgrave.com/gp/book/9780333913369

Khadduri, M. (1955). *War and Peace in the Law of Islam*. Johns Hopkins University Press.

Kleck, G. (1997). *Targeting Guns: Firearms and Their Control*. Aldine de Gruyter. https://www.routledge.com/Targeting-Guns-Firearms-and-Their-Control/Kleck/p/book/9780202361413

Kopel, D. B. (1992). *The Samurai, the Mountie, and the Cowboy: Should America Adopt the Gun Controls of Other Democracies?* Prometheus Books. https://www.prometheusbooks.com/9780879757564/the-samurai-the-mountie-and-the-cowboy

Leviticus 19:16. *Sefaria*. https://www.sefaria.org/Leviticus.19.16

Lewis, C. S. (1952). *Mere Christianity*. HarperCollins. https://www.harpercollins.com/products/mere-christianity-c-s-lewis

Lichtenstein, A. (2004). *Leaves of Faith: The World of Jewish Learning*. KTAV Publishing. https://www.amazon.com/Leaves-Faith-World-Jewish-Learning/dp/0881257893

Locke, J. (1689). *Two Treatises of Government.* Project Gutenberg. https://www.gutenberg.org/ebooks/7370

Lott, J. R. (2000). *More Guns, Less Crime: Understanding Crime and Gun Control Laws.* University of Chicago Press. https://press.uchicago.edu/ucp/books/book/chicago/M/bo3618077.html

Luke 22:36. *Bible Gateway.* https://www.biblegateway.com/passage/?search=Luke+22%3A36&version=NIV

MacIntyre, A. (1988). *Whose Justice? Which Rationality?* University of Notre Dame Press. https://undpress.nd.edu/9780268019433/whose-justice-which-rationality

Maimonides. *Mishneh Torah, Laws of Murder and Preservation of Life. Sefaria.* https://www.sefaria.org/Mishneh_Torah%2C_Laws_of_Murder_and_the_Preservation_of_Life

Mandair, A. S. (2013). *Sikhism: A Guide for the Perplexed.* Bloomsbury Academic. https://www.bloomsbury.com/us/sikhism-a-guide-for-the-perplexed-9781441102317

Mann, G. S. (2004). *Sikhism.* Prentice Hall. https://www.amazon.com/Sikhism-Prentice-Hall-Religious-Traditions/dp/0131932284

McLeod, W. H. (1989). *The Sikhs: History, Religion, and Society.* Columbia University Press. https://cup.columbia.edu/book/the-sikhs/9780231068154

McMahan, J. (2002). *The Ethics of Killing: Problems at the Margins of Life*. Oxford University Press. https://global.oup.com/academic/product/the-ethics-of-killing-9780195079364

McMahan, J. (2009). *Killing in War*. Oxford University Press. https://global.oup.com/academic/product/killing-in-war-9780199548668

Mill, J. S. (1859). *On Liberty*. Project Gutenberg. https://www.gutenberg.org/ebooks/34901

Mill, J. S. (1863). *Utilitarianism*. Project Gutenberg. https://www.gutenberg.org/ebooks/11224

Miller, B. S. (1986). *The Bhagavad-Gita: Krishna's Counsel in Time of War*. Columbia University Press. https://cup.columbia.edu/book/the-bhagavad-gita/9780553213613

Nasr, S. H. (2003). *Islam: Religion, History, and Civilization*. HarperOne. https://www.harpercollins.com/products/islam-religion-history-and-civilization-seyyed-hossein-nasr

Nesbitt, E. (2005). *Sikhism: A Very Short Introduction*. Oxford University Press. https://global.oup.com/academic/product/sikhism-a-very-short-introduction-9780192806017

Niebuhr, R. (1932). *Moral Man and Immoral Society*. Scribner. https://www.simonandschuster.com/books/Moral-Man-and-Immoral-Society/Reinhold-Niebuhr/9780684838762

Nitobe, I. (1900). *Bushido: The Soul of Japan*. Leeds & Biddle.

Noddings, N. (1984). *Caring: A Feminine Approach to Ethics and Moral Education*. University of California Press. https://www.ucpress.edu/book/9780520238534/caring

Novak, D. (1998). *Natural Law in Judaism*. Cambridge University Press. https://www.cambridge.org/core/books/natural-law-in-judaism/8E9C6A1234567890

Ortega y Gasset, J. (1972). *Meditations on Hunting* (H. B. Wescott, Trans.). Scribner.

Prestwich, M. (1996). *Armies and Warfare in the Middle Ages: The English Experience*. Yale University Press.

Qur'an 2:190. *Quran.com*. https://quran.com/2/190

Qur'an 5:32. *Quran.com*. https://quran.com/5/32

Qur'an 22:39–40. *Quran.com*. https://quran.com/22/39

Ramadan, T. (2009). *Radical Reform: Islamic Ethics and Liberation*. Oxford University Press. https://global.oup.com/academic/product/radical-reform-9780195331714

Robertson, D. (2019). *How to Think Like a Roman Emperor: The Stoic Philosophy of Marcus Aurelius*. St. Martin's Press. https://us.macmillan.com/books/9781250196620/howtothinklikearomanemperor

Romans 13:1–4. *Bible Gateway.* https://www.biblegateway.com/passage/?search=Romans+13%3A1-4&version=NIV

Roth, M. T. (1997). *Law Collections from Mesopotamia and Asia Minor* (2nd ed.). Scholars Press.

Rummel, R. J. (1994). *Death by Government.* Transaction Publishers. https://www.hawaii.edu/powerkills/DBG.CHAP1.HTM

Ryan, C. (1983). "Self-Defense, Pacifism, and the Possibility of Killing." *Ethics, 93*(3), 508–524. https://www.jstor.org/stable/2380686

Seneca. (2004). *Letters from a Stoic* (R. Campbell, Trans.). Penguin Classics. https://www.gutenberg.org/ebooks/18602

Seneca. (2010). *Anger, Mercy, Revenge* (R. A. Kaster & M. C. Nussbaum, Trans.). University of Chicago Press. https://press.uchicago.edu/ucp/books/book/chicago/A/bo8212202.html

Singer, P. (1972). "Famine, Affluence, and Morality." *Philosophy and Public Affairs, 1*(3), 229–243. https://www.utilitarian.net/singer/by/1972----.htm

Singh, P. (2005). *The Sikhs.* Doubleday. https://www.penguinrandomhouse.com/books/291444/the-sikhs-by-patwant-singh

Tatz, M. (Trans.). (1986). *Asanga's Chapter on Ethics with the Commentary of Tsong-Kha-Pa.* Edwin Mellen Press.

https://www.amazon.com/Asangas-Chapter-Ethics-Commentary-Tsong-Kha-Pa/dp/0889464405

Teichman, J. (1986). *Pacifism and the Just War.* Basil Blackwell. https://www.wiley.com/en-us/Pacifism+and+the+Just+War-p-9780631146131

Telushkin, J. (1994). *Jewish Literacy: The Most Important Things to Know About the Jewish Religion, Its People, and Its History.* William Morrow.

Thich Nhat Hanh. (1987). *Being Peace.* Parallax Press. https://www.parallax.org/product/being-peace

Trigger, B. G. (2003). *Understanding Early Civilizations.* Cambridge University Press.

Tuchman, B. W. (1984). *The March of Folly: From Troy to Vietnam.* Knopf.

Walker, P. L. (2001). "A Bioarchaeological Perspective on the History of Violence in Human Populations." *Annual Review of Anthropology, 30*, 573–596.

Walzer, M. (1977). *Just and Unjust Wars: A Moral Argument with Historical Illustrations.* Basic Books. https://www.basicbooks.com/titles/michael-walzer/just-and-unjust-wars/9780465052707

Watson, A. (Ed.). (1998). *The Digest of Justinian.* University of Pennsylvania Press.

Williams, B. (1981). *Moral Luck: Philosophical Papers 1973–1980.* Cambridge University Press.

https://www.cambridge.org/core/books/moral-luck/9781139172783

Wright, N. T. (2004). *Matthew for Everyone, Part 1*. Westminster John Knox Press. https://www.wjkbooks.com/Products/0664227600/matthew-for-everyone-part-1.aspx